Famous for its miles of beaches, lighthouses, farmland, and sea-food, Prince Edward Island is a destination for travelers and food lovers alike. Nestled on forty-six acres of land overlooking the picturesque Fortune River near the eastern tip of Prince Edward Island, the Inn at Bay Fortune is a leading five-star country inn with the award-winning restaurant FireWorks offering a unique live-fire culinary experience with unforgettable meals enjoyed family-style at long feast tables.

The Inn at Bay Fortune is first an organic farm, encompassing eight fertile acres, multiple herb gardens, various permanent farm beds, five greenhouses, and a small orchard. As a restaurant with its own farm, award-winning chef Michael Smith brings his culinary knowledge and passion for flavour to the restaurant and this stunning collection of recipes inspired by the ingredients of the Island and cooking with multiple fires daily to pull off the FireWorks Feast.

Featuring gorgeous food and location photography, *Farm, Fire & Feast* is an impressive cookbook. Smith's collection of unique recipes includes Iron-Seared Island Scallops, Oven-Baked Salt-Crusted Halibut, Beach Lobster, Wood-Grilled Butcher's Steak, Smokehouse Pork Belly, Wood-Roasted Spatchcock Chicken and Vegetables, Fire Garden Tacos, Sunchoke Fries, Potato Bacon Cheddar Tart, Strawberry Rhubarb Shortcake, and Wild Blueberry Maple Grunt. Packed with recipes to cook over fire, wherever possible, alternative cooking methods are provided so a recipe can be pulled off in an indoor kitchen—and all are well within the reach of the home cook.

MICHAEL SMITH

FARM, FIRE & FEAST

Recipes from the Inn at Bay Fortune

PENGUIN
an imprint of Penguin Canada, a division of Penguin Random House Canada Limited

Canada • USA • UK • Ireland • Australia • New Zealand • India • South Africa • China

First published 2021

www.penguinrandomhouse.ca

Library and Archives Canada Cataloguing in Publication

Title: Farm, fire and feast : recipes from the Inn at Bay Fortune / Michael Smith
Names: Smith, Michael, 1966 October 13- author.
Identifiers: Canadiana (print) 20200237888 | Canadiana (ebook) 20200237896 |
    ISBN 9780735233843 (hardcover) | ISBN 9780735233850 (EPUB)
Subjects: LCSH: Cooking, Canadian—Maritime Provinces style. | LCSH: Cooking—Prince Edward Island. |
    LCGFT: Cookbooks.
Classification: LCC TX715.6 .S5825 2021 | DDC 641.59717—dc23

Cover and book design: Terri Nimmo
Cover and interior photography: Al Douglas

Printed and bound in China

10 9 8 7 6 5 4 3 2 1

Penguin
Random House
PENGUIN CANADA

Dedicated to all who break bread at
the Inn at Bay Fortune.

We gather, prepare, and share
our best for you.

CONTENTS

FOREWORD

BY TODD PERRIN

I met Michael Smith on Prince Edward Island about twenty-five years ago when I was a not-so-young but very impressionable student at the Culinary Institute of Canada's Holland College. I was there with some other culinary students. Together, we had been conscripted to help with a charity event featuring some of Prince Edward Island's best-known chefs.

Michael's crew was tasked with building a couple hundred salads, each consisting of dozens of ingredients deftly placed inside a rye crouton cracker tube, but I wasn't part of that group. Instead, I helped Chef Stefan Czapaly shuck hundreds of oysters and deep-fry sage leaves sandwiched between gossamer-thin potato slices for the potato oyster chests we were creating. Chef Stefan led the brigade superbly in the execution of our dish, but there was something magnetic about the way Michael strode around the kitchen and worked with the crew to create his own culinary wonder. Each leaf in the salad was precisely placed in its assigned spot, with herbs adding layers of flavour and texture. He exuded a focus I had never seen before. In his eyes, I could see his determination to make a dish that would wow the crowd with its innovation and flavour.

For many years that was my impression of Michael—the larger-than-life chef at the event I worked in college. Of course, Michael went on to become one of the best-known chefs anywhere, with multiple television shows, cookbooks, and sold-out events to his name.

When I finished cooking school, my own career took several turns. After years of unfulfilled dreams, I got the chance to do some food television. My appearance on the first season of *Top Chef Canada* brought Michael and I back into each other's orbit. Michael asked me to join him and a great group of pan-Canadian chefs at a huge event in Fort McMurray, Alberta. I was excited that he had given me the chance to join his crew, and doubly excited because I was in the last stage of renovating Mallard Cottage—my dream restaurant in a 200-year-old cottage in Quidi Vidi Village, St. John's, Newfoundland. What could be better marketing for my new venture, I figured, than to be a part of an event in the only city in Canada with more resident Newfoundlanders and Labradorians than St. John's?

While prepping for the event with the assembled throng of chefs, I got a call from home. Mallard Cottage was on fire! My dream was potentially going up in smoke and I was practically on the other side of the country. Mallard Cottage didn't burn down, but it was substantially damaged. Being so far away, I felt lucky that I was with a group of chefs whose empathy and support I desperately needed. Michael in particular gave me several pep talks: "You've got this. You've built something special there. Why don't you go home and fix it?"

So, that's just what I did. We fixed the damage and got the restaurant up and running. When it came time to invite our first guest chef, there was no question about who we would ask. Michael generously accepted our invitation and became the reason we had our first sold-out event at Mallard Cottage. I was proud to share my dream with the chef who had inspired me from the first time I met him—in ways that he did not even know.

I got to share my dream with Michael and in this book I believe he is sharing his dream with the world. *Farm, Fire & Feast* is the accumulation of over thirty years of cooking, listening, tasting, and learning. It often takes cooks and chefs many years to realize the simple truth that less is more. Here, Michael embraces the idea as he returns to the alchemy of land and fire. In addition, he reveals the deep love he has for his home by paying respect to the local farmers, fishermen, foragers, brewers, distillers, bakers, and butchers—all those who have built Prince Edward Island's reputation as Canada's food island.

With his return to the restaurant kitchen at the Inn at Bay Fortune, Michael brings us to the table with hunger and curiosity: hunger for wonderful food, cultivated with love, care and purpose; curiosity about the story he will weave from the land and ingredients that surround him. Even more powerful, is the connection he creates between people and their food: where it comes from, how it gets to them, and how precious it actually is. He grows and serves food at the Inn at Bay Fortune, but what Michael truly cultivates is love and appreciation for the land, sea, and food, all wrapped up together.

As the Greek philosopher Epicurus said, "We should look for someone to eat and drink with before looking for something to eat and drink." Lucky for us, Michael provides both.

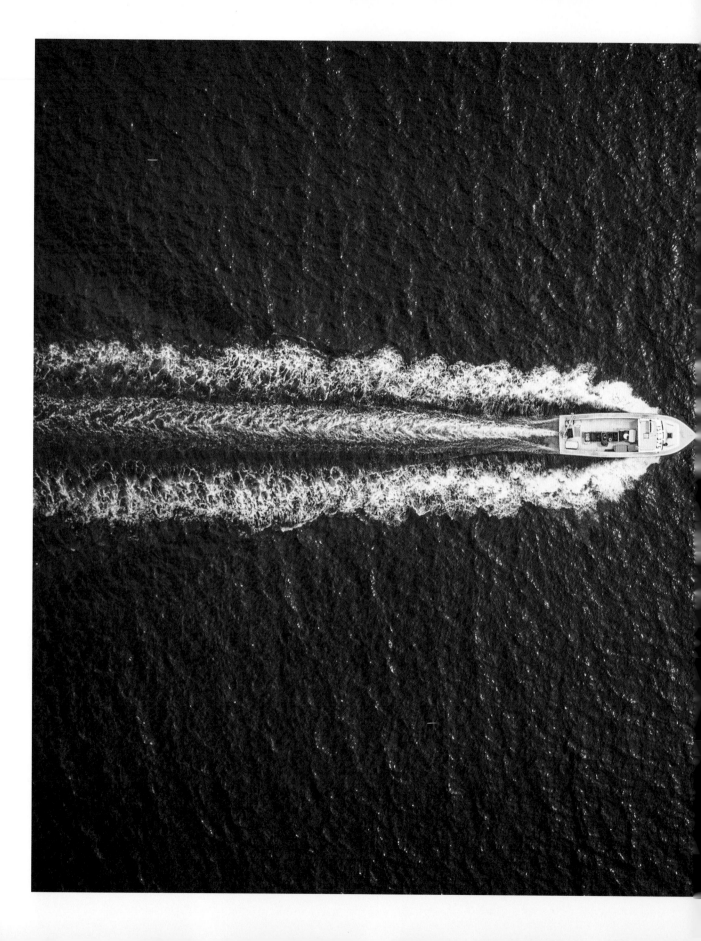

INTRODUCTION

Fortune, Prince Edward Island, has long been a community of hard-working farmers, fisherfolk, and colourful artists nestled around Bay Fortune and the picturesque Fortune River near the eastern tip of the island. In the late 1800s the river was legendary for some of the very best sport fishing in North America. Word reached Broadway, which shut down in the summer before air conditioning was invented. Hordes of out-of-work artists thought a seaside retreat was worth a long journey, so a summer colony of sorts formed along the bay overlooking the Northumberland Strait towards the Atlantic Ocean beyond. In 1910, playwright Elmer Harris was a Broadway legend when he built his cottage on the island. He was careful to include a guest wing for his entourage who would stay for months at a time. A tall tower was built to support a large water tank to create water pressure for his modern plumbing. Over the years that tower became a local landmark.

Several owners and many years later, the Wilmer family saw potential in the long-vacant, dilapidated property and tackled a full renovation. The Inn at Bay Fortune welcomed its first guests in 1989. It has been open ever since, from May to October each year.

In 1992, I was a Culinary Institute of America grad and an apprentice chef in one of the finest French restaurants in New York City. My time in a few fine-dining temples in London and New York had already ignited my passion for great ingredients, but I sensed there was more. I wanted to "meet some farmers and plant a garden." I had no idea what those words really meant when I bet the farm, loaded my old jeep to the scuppers, and headed for a remote island.

I discovered a paradise. A multi-hued bright green patchwork of flavours, fertile soil, fresh ingredients both familiar and obscure, world-class fresh fish, passionate farmers, and a network of farmers' markets.

I arrived at the Inn at Bay Fortune for the property's fourth season. As the new chef, I immediately established an herb garden and a small specialty vegetable plot. During my initial seven-year tenure, I tracked down and used in my menus every single ingredient produced on the island, and our experimental kitchen gained an international reputation for regionally inspired cooking. We helped ignite a respect for the ingredients of the island that endures in its many restaurants today.s

After seventeen years away from the stoves at the inn focusing on writing books and cooking shows opportunity knocked yet again. In 2015, with my wife, Chastity, we debuted the newly imagined property as proprietors, and I returned to my roots as a chef. We fully renovated, imaginatively redecorated, and creatively relaunched as one of the world's most authentic culinary destinations and Prince Edward Island's leading five-star country inn. We define ourselves through three simple words: Farm, Fire, and Feast.

Somewhere driving up and down all those red clay lanes on the island, I learned the biggest lesson of my career—a human being created each impeccable ingredient that makes our kitchen great. The respect we show our ingredients is personal as we celebrate our friends' work. As cooks, we know we are mere intermediaries, elevating the ingredients we source from our farmers and fisherfolk to serve our guests. We share our producers' stories through our cooking.

And it all begins on our own culinary farm.

Our Culinary Farm

The Inn at Bay Fortune is first a farm. We grow what we serve, yet we harvest far more than impeccable produce from our soil. Our culinary farm, led by farmer Kevin Petrie and chef de cuisine Chris Gibb, encompasses eight fertile acres, multiple herb gardens, various permanent farm beds, five greenhouses, a small orchard, and an ever-growing knowledge of our unique ecosystem.

As our farm has matured, our own distinctive terroir has emerged. You can sense the vitality as you wander the rows; you can smell the primal health of the earth and you can see it in the plants. Best of all, you can taste it. We've developed our own particular flavour, subtle at first but gaining strength with time. It's something more than ripeness or freshness. It's our own terroir, and it has become powerful enough to add real intensity to our farm's flavours.

Our culinary farm shares the island landscape with large commercial monoculture farms, smaller market-garden farms, single-family subsistence farms, vineyards, orchards, dairy farms, livestock farms, and even fish farms. Each has an integrity of its own, yet our focus is particularly challenging.

Flavour First

As a restaurant with its own farm, we are naturally focused on flavour. Because our ingredients are harvested perfectly ripe and served impeccably fresh, they taste amazing. Our harvest is not chemically encouraged or picked underripe so it can survive a long trip to market. Nevertheless, there's a lot more to learn about flavour and a lot more to a farm than just its harvest.

Regenerative Agriculture

As farmers we understand that our first responsibility is to our soil, to the earth around us. We naturally focus on the life of our plants, but they come and go while the life of the soil endures. Our systems continuously strengthen the incredibly diverse and productive microorganisms within that soil. Organic is just our starting line. With one foot planted in the past and another firmly in the future, we deploy a wide array of fascinating natural techniques to ensure long-term vitality. We're inspired by the circle of life: the ongoing connection between healthy soil, a healthy environment, and healthy, happy humans. We know that the better an ingredient tastes, the better it is for you, and the better the earth it came from.

Life Cycle Harvesting

One of the most fascinating aspects of culinary farming is being a part of the plant's life from start to finish. We learn respect from the hard work of nurturing the seed all the way through to harvest, but we also find creative inspiration and new flavours every step of the way. So many of our plants are unexpectedly delicious throughout their life cycle, offering many distinct flavours and textures as they grow, and often different parts of the plant than are traditionally harvested or long after the traditional crop has been harvested. Most important, we've learned to instinctively regard our ingredients as alive, not static or dead.

Diversity

One of our farm's purposes is to offer our chefs and guests as many different ingredients and flavours as possible. We grow multiple varietals of every vegetable we can, every herb we can source, and as many types as possible—both the obvious and the obscure—hundreds of different plants every season and new ones every year. Our chefs love creating with new flavours, while our guests appreciate the amazing variety and the many new ingredients they've never encountered before. And our farm benefits from the diversity, too, since each plant brings its own particular strengths to our ever-growing ecosystem.

Innovation

We are a living laboratory, not limited by normal farming constraints. Our continuous improvement and eyes-open approach encourage experimentation. The overwhelming diversity around us is an ever-present reminder that there's always a better way. Every season we improve what we already do. Every year we add a laundry list of new plants to the mix and always introduce a new challenge: an early-season herb house, tender microgreens and seed sprouts, cultivated mushrooms, egg-laying chickens, a windmill, a solar power grid, closed-loop mariponic systems producing plants from living fish effluent, the list goes on.

Education

Our farm gives us far more than food. Every day we learn more and more from our soil. In turn, we share that knowledge every way we can. It's part of our DNA. A day on our farm begins with the entire chef's brigade and their daily Farm Project. Ten cooks can get a lot done in one hour, and we love starting our day on the farm. As our farmer leads the way, we tackle a task or two and learn something new. This shared time of toil and triumph has inspired many a budding culinary career. Later, the sun slips away and the day ends with a well-attended farm tour as our guests spend an hour absorbing the intricacies of culinary farming. Their conversation continues well into the evening and beyond as our farm feeds the body, mind, and soul.

Wood, Fire, Flame, and Smoke

I grew up around fires. Warm wood stoves, big bonfires, random campfires, and toasted marshmallows were a big part of my life. During my first tenure at the inn in the 1990s, though, we cooked with a standard North American gas-fired range. My love of fire was largely expressed after work, on nearby Back Beach. During my seventeen years away from restaurant stoves, something ignited in me. I built a wood oven and a small hearth in my home and I learned how to use them through lots of trial and error. As my family's cook, I got lots of practice with my back deck's Big Green Egg and backyard fire pit. Every food writer knew my favourite meal was a thick steak grilled over a bed of glowing hardwood coals, enjoyed with friends. When opportunity knocked, I immediately knew our new inn would be fire-driven. I just didn't know what that meant yet.

The Woodpile

Every year we burn forty-five cords of local hardwood that we've seasoned for at least two years. That's an immense amount. Our woodpile is legendary. (One cord equals a pile of split, stacked wood four feet high, four feet wide, and eight feet long.) Truckloads of eight-foot maple and birch logs are harvested within ten kilometres of our fires. We block the logs with chainsaws into eighteen-inch lengths, split them into smaller pieces, and carefully stack the works in long, long lines. Then we wait patiently for Mother Nature and Father Time to dry out the wood. We've learned that seasoned wood is much lighter to handle, burns far hotter, and produces a tastier, more flavourful smoke that's easier on our chimneys. We've learned to prefer the smoke of maple over birch, but rely on both for hot fires. We reserve scarce apple, cherry, and alder wood for our smokehouse, because their smoke is particularly fragrant. We avoid burning softwoods like pine and spruce indoors, since their resinous smoke clogs our chimneys. We love softwood outdoors, though, where it burns fast and furious. We've also learned the most important lesson of all: when the folks who burn the wood also split and stack the wood, somehow we burn less wood.

Twelve Fires

It takes at least twelve fires a day to pull off the FireWorks Feast. Many of those fires burn in our custom-built fire kitchen. The first is built in our wood oven after we bake bread in the retained heat of the last fire of the day; every night we build the biggest fire of the day in the oven, seal it up, and leave it till morning. Our centrepiece hearth also has a life of its own as various fierce fires come and go all day long. The smokehouse is slower, as we carefully nurture a smouldering fire throughout the day, bathing beef brisket, pork bellies, ribs, salmon sides, and other culinary projects with hours of slow, smoky goodness. All of this happens indoors under the careful watch of our Fire Marshal.

The Fire Garden

In the great outdoors we're unrestrained by the limits of mortgages, insurance policies, and fine print. We're not reckless, but over the years we've accumulated a vast collection of fire-driven ideas that we feature during oyster hour as our guests wander our whimsical grounds. We can build a fire anywhere, but prefer it up off the ground for ease and effect. Each fire has a specific purpose and thus specific characteristics. We grill, char, smoke, sear, roast, toast, steam, and simmer daily. Just when you think you've seen it all, we even build a roaring campfire for toasting marshmallows.

Fast Flaming Heat and Slow Wood Smoke

Our first season with the FireWorks was spent trying to emulate the precision of gas in the kitchens I was used to. We fumbled our way along, cooked a lot of tasty food, and even learned a few things. In our second season we survived a few juvenile challenges and learned a few more things. One night during our third season, though, it hit me like a bolt of proverbial lightning: we have more than a gas kitchen at our fingertips. We have controllable heat on a scale unlike that from any gas appliance. We harness and deploy a spectrum of wood-fired heat, from searing flames to thick, glowing coal beds to warm wood ovens. We know how to be ready when we need to be. We understand the ease of fast fires and have mastered the challenges of slower, smokier ones.

The Fire Code

I've spent my life around fires and good food, so I've heard a few stories and learned a few lessons. The craft of the fire. The art of the cooking. Respect for safety as my constant companion. Wood smoke is addictively delicious. People are drawn to fires. Drying wood for years and tending a fire for many hours for mere moments of flavour seems perfectly natural. With these lessons I've cracked the code of the crackling flame.

There is only the way of the flame. Zen is within the art and craft of wood-fired cookery. Calm and quiet is found in the flames, because to harness fire requires absolute focus. You have to be present—for safety, of course, but also for the active creation and control of heat. There are so many constant variables that you have to pay attention. It's so seductive. Addictive even. Hours flash by in seconds. It's hard work, but it's tremendously rewarding. And you smell really good.

Precision Fire

Live-fire cooking is tremendously rewarding and equally challenging. Every step of the way, multiple variables impede consistency. It's just part of the game. The recipes in this book are useful guidelines, but your own contribution is equally important. You know your fires best. Read between the lines and trust your gut. With fire on the menu, safety always comes first. We also embrace modern digital technology to help us accurately gauge time and temperature. See page 11 for my suggested Fire Pit Kit.

The FireWorks Feast

We have so many things to be proud of at the Inn at Bay Fortune. Chastity and I and our team have worked hard to build something special. The inn has become a key part of our community, and we are thrilled to support an ever-growing roster of passionate farmers, fisherfolk, and culinary artisans. We've watched our team grow and mature and are humbled by their embrace. We've created an epic farm and we harvest real knowledge from it. Our fires burn brighter every day. The one thing we're most proud of, though, is not ours. It belongs to our guests. Humanity.

In 2015, as we spent a long winter renovating the property and building the FireWorks, we imagined what kind of restaurant we'd like to be. The first two big, broad brushstrokes were easy: let's grow what we serve and let's cook it all with live fire. Who wouldn't want to go to a place like that? The last idea was scary, though. We didn't want to create a normal fine-dining restaurant and be tied to the rules of the à la carte world I had left behind. If we were going to farm, the harvest of the day had to lead the way. We needed our guests to trust us and we wanted to get them out of their seats too. Gradually my idea formed for a shared feast. An entire life spent celebrating the joy of the table rewarded me with the biggest and scariest idea of all: let's seat everybody together at the same time for a once-a-night communal meal.

Nobody got it. I barely got it. I'd never heard of such a place. There was nowhere to go and see how they did it. All I had was my gut feeling that all the family meals I had cooked for so many years meant something. I didn't sleep a lot that winter, and it didn't help when word leaked on the front page of our local newspaper what we were up to. Our first phone call was from a long-time guest cancelling reservations and berating us for ruining what had made the inn special. "Strangers sitting with strangers," they harrumphed. "Imagine!" But we stuck to our guns and somehow opened on time.

Our first night of service was a blur as we discovered all the things we didn't know yet. At the end of the night, though, I knew one thing for sure. Our guests were having the time of their lives. It was a great big raucous kitchen party. They were getting along fabulously. Something was happening that was much bigger than farm-fresh food and live-fire cooking. Two couples that had just met made reservations to return together on the same day the next year. I went home and slept like a baby.

In the years since, we've created from scratch the systems we need to run our special restaurant and we've figured out the intricacies of service. We now know what we are most proud of. Human beings are at our best when we gather with friends and family around food. It's in us. At our long butcher-block tables our guests come alive as they instinctively set aside their differences and remember that they're just people together at a table and sharing. They give thanks, break bread, tell stories, and enjoy a meal together. Without realizing it, they remind themselves of what it is to be a human being.

A NOTE ABOUT THE RECIPES
AND COOKING WITH FIRE

Yields

Most of the recipes in this book make enough for a normal meal for an average-sized family. The intricate restaurant-style fish and dessert plates are designed for dinner parties of eight, and you'll end up with some leftovers here and there. It's impractical if not impossible to make smaller amounts with some of the more elaborate techniques. No worries, though—all the leftovers will be delicious.

Substitute Ingredients

Many of the ingredients are unique to our farm and to Prince Edward Island. Some are foraged wild. For the more obscure ingredients, whenever possible, a substitution is suggested. The results won't be the same, of course, but they will be enjoyable in their own way. In some cases, though, there just isn't any viable option. If you're interested in tracking down the real thing, see Special Ingredients and Contacts on page 255.

Alternative Techniques

Live-fire cooking requires lots of resources, outdoor space, and time. It's not the sort of thing easily done in every backyard or on a condo balcony. Wherever possible, alternative measures are suggested so a recipe can be pulled off in an indoor kitchen. No liquid smoke, though!

Animal Fats

Our style of cooking is both plant-based and nose-to-tail. One of its hallmarks is the judicious use of animal fats. Like any good kitchen, we prefer not to waste resources, so we carefully save the various fats that come our way, mainly pork, beef, chicken, and duck. A few drops in a vegetable dish can add lots of deliciousness without the heaviness of meat itself. At home we often enjoy an entire meatless meal except for a bit of animal fat in one dish. Of course, these are optional ingredients, and for our vegetarian friends easily omitted.

Complexity

I am a chef, and some of my techniques are elaborately technical. They're accurately described here. If you choose to tackle them, I suggest you enjoy the process as much as the resulting flavours. But I also do things at work that I'd never do at home, so wherever possible I've suggested simpler techniques that yield equally impressive results.

Presentation

We all enjoy beautifully presented and great-tasting food, a feast for our eyes as much as our bellies. As chefs, we show respect for our ingredients and our guests by taking the time to make our presentations as beautiful as possible. Throughout the recipes you'll find various presentation tips and even specific steps to follow if you're plating like we do at the inn.

Fire Pit Kit

The many methods of live-fire cooking require a specialized set of tools, some ancient, some modern. Like any fire kitchen, we've custom built many of our tools, but many come straight off the shelf. Over time you'll build up your own arsenal too. Here's a list to get you started:

- Heavy-duty work gloves for handling live fire
- Handheld digital thermometer (essential)
- App-enabled remote thermometer for your smartphone (optional)
- Long, sturdy tongs
- Heavy-duty grilles
- Cast-iron skillets, griddles, and planchas
- Pokers or thick sticks, 4 feet (1.2 metres) long or so
- Flat-bottom shovel or spade
- 4 pieces of rebar, each 3 to 4 feet (1 to 1.2 metres) long
- Stack of firebricks and cinder blocks
- A friendly local metalshop

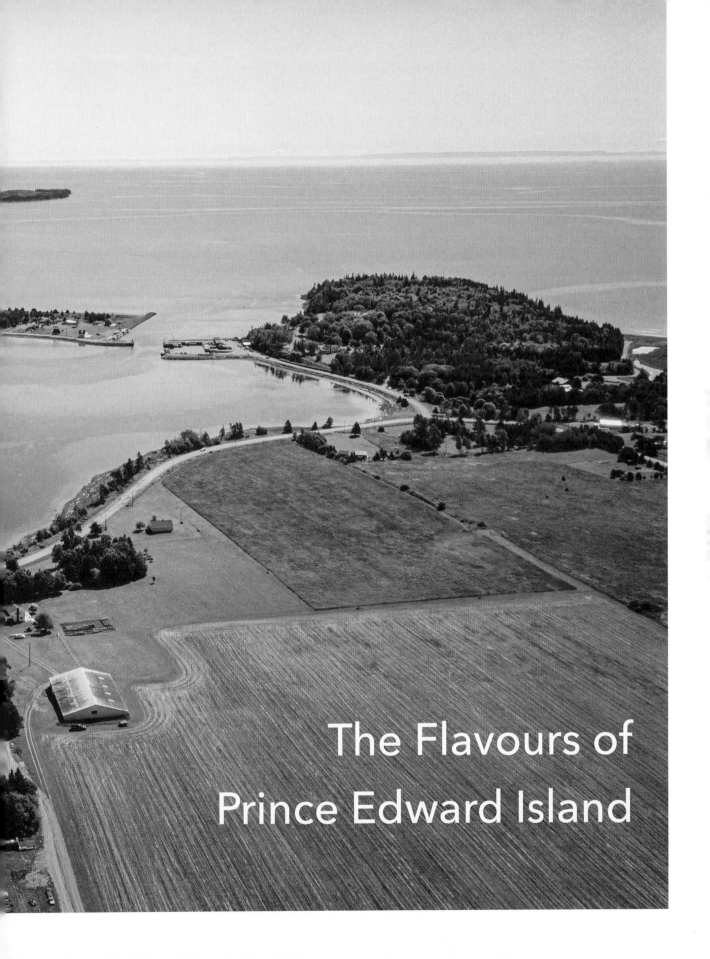

The Flavours of
Prince Edward Island

OVERWINTERED SUNCHOKES

Many Indigenous cultures in North America were already cultivating the delicious wild sunchoke (also known as Jerusalem artichoke) long before Samuel de Champlain and other Europeans arrived and discovered its mild flavour and sweetness for themselves. For a thousand years the easily grown and harvested vegetable was a subsistence staple on and around Prince Edward Island and across the continent. Now this distinctive vegetable is a star member of our culinary farm.

Our sunchokes have a well-established bed of their own along one windswept edge of our farm. The hearty plants are perfectly adapted to our maritime climate. Over the years, a thick, permanent bed of roots and tubers has formed. Every year a new thicket of tall stalks and sun-seeking flowers adds more strength to the thick root mass below. The plants are so strong that they form a tough windbreak along the northern edge of the farm. Like so many plants prized by humans, they spend summer storing the sun's energy as sugar in their roots. Farmers long ago discovered that the tubers were delectable year-round but tasted even better if they were left in the earth all winter long. With time their sugars convert into pure fructose and the roots become even tastier.

Sunchokes are one of our early-season staples. Their flavour and texture are so similar to potato that they help anchor our meat courses until we can start digging new potatoes. Then we leave the bed alone until the next spring. We can't seem to make a dent in it, though. For every four or five tubers we dig out, we leave one behind. That's more than enough to keep this bed thriving.

Sunchokes have a well-earned reputation as the single most flatulence-inducing vegetable known to humankind. Fortunately, the dramatic effect is louder than it is aromatic, and it's easily mitigated by overwintering the vegetable. That gives the offending carbohydrate the time it needs to convert into pure, easily absorbed, tasty fructose.

WILD WATERCRESS

Every forager's surrounding environment is unique. On Prince Edward Island, the first wild flavour of the year is always watercress. (Also see photo on page 18.) The leaves have a sweet, crisp lettuce-like flavour and its pleasing peppery vibrance is a bright green start to the season and an annual reminder of the foraging ahead. Wild watercress can also be dramatic. Since streambeds form gullies, they can fill in with deep snowdrifts. As the melt begins and the hidden stream starts flowing, this hearty plant springs to life. If you know where to look, you'll find cool fresh watercress and pure white snow together.

Watercress grows prolifically in the fresh running water of island streambeds. The common aquatic plant has hollow stems, ingeniously allowing the leaves to float on the water. Its tenacity can be challenging for dry-feet-loving foragers, though. Wandering through woods and fields bending over now and then is one thing. Perilously leaning over a running stream is another. Good boots and good balance are essential.

Wild watercress season lasts for six weeks or so. Towards the end of the season, as our floating patch strains to reproduce, each day the plants relentlessly form spicy yellow flowers that we just as relentlessly harvest. Eventually Mother Nature prevails, and the plant moves past its vegetative state to its reproductive stage. But before we give up, we are rewarded with a week or so of these tasty wild watercress flowers.

Whether you're knee deep in a stream or sitting at a dining table, watercress is a real treat raw. Its freshness is fleeting, so during the season we forage our favourite streams every day. The snappy leaves are an excellent early-season addition to our salad mix or a sharp contrast to equally seasonal lobster. Watercress can also be briefly blanched, then puréed into a bright green sauce.

RHUBARB HILL

Rhubarb was one of the treasures Marco Polo sought along the Silk Road to the Far East. He found it growing in the mountains of northern China, where it had been a vital medicinal plant for thousands of years. The perennial vegetable made its way to Europe and eventually North America. Somewhere along the way it became a fruit. (To cooks, anyway, but botanists think differently.)

Now rhubarb thrives in cool climes all over the world. On Prince Edward Island we have beds that are more than a hundred years old. One nearby hillside below a long-abandoned barn, with the rich soil of its long-gone livestock, is so thickly covered with wild plants that it's known as Rhubarb Hill. It's a treasured part of many families' food stories. (Also see photo on page 19.)

On Rhubarb Hill an informal harvest code protects the plants. The land hasn't been farmed for years, and the owner doesn't mind the annual influx of harvesters. There's enough for everybody, and we're all careful not to take more than our fair share. When the first tender crimson stalks emerge in June, I'm there waiting. In the first few days we'll harvest a few here and there but not enough to slow down the patch. Better to let the plants strengthen a bit, so we wait patiently. This gives other folks a chance to begin harvesting too. We all know to go easy until after the patch's annual star turn.

Every summer our community hosts the Village Feast, a gigantic steak dinner fundraiser for a thousand guests that features the flavours of the Island. We wait for our local berries, so dessert is always Strawberry Rhubarb Shortcake (page 221). Since the two iconic ingredients' seasons don't overlap, a team of volunteers heads out a month before the event to harvest a hundred pounds from Rhubarb Hill. We stew it simply, with sugar, then freeze it for the big day. Then it's fair game to hit the hill for a larger harvest.

To harvest rhubarb, locate its crown under the canopy of the plant. At ground level you'll find where the stalks meet. Grasp a larger one with both hands and firmly pull up from the roots. With practice it will snap off cleanly and not damage the plant. Trim off and discard the broad leaf. Never take all the stalks from one plant. A well-established plant can easily yield two or three stalks a day for six weeks. Eventually the plant will send up a tall flower stalk, and the harvest will end.

FORTUNE WHARF SHE LOBSTER

The world of food is full of iconic flavours. Wherever you are on the globe, a handful of local ingredients always come to define a place. On Prince Edward Island, the list is led by our world-famous lobster. No other commodity is as lucrative or as deeply ingrained in our community. The ways of our fisherfolk define us all. We celebrate their success and mourn their tragedies. It's the Island way. We also eat as much of the catch as we can.

The Inn at Bay Fortune is a five-minute stroll from the historic Fortune wharf. Our little bay enjoys open access to the rich seas of Northumberland Strait and a protected inner harbour sheltering twenty state-of-the-art lobster boats. During the brief two-month annual season—May and June—the wharf is the centre of our community. A 4 A.M. rush hour starts the day as the fisherfolk take advantage of the calm pre-dawn seas. A day and 272 traps later—every single one hoisted from the seabed, opened, emptied, sorted, rebaited, and reset—they sail for home.

The Atlantic Canadian lobster fishery is regulated to protect our vital and tasty resource. Our fisherfolk and scientists are proud to work together. Big business follows suit. As islanders and responsible cooks, we're proud to be waiting when the boats return, rain or shine. Over the years many, many cooks have run down to the wharf to get the fish. It's a ritual, a real chance to connect with the people behind an important ingredient. Only that human connection leads to true respect for our ingredients.

During May and June, we serve lobster every single night to every single guest—unless they're allergic, of course. That's a lot of lobster. Thousands of pounds fresh. We hand-select large female lobsters directly off the boat. We prefer to have the females' tasty eggs as an extra ingredient for our guests. We fill a standard-issue fish pan with their squirming, vaguely violent living mass, often fifty lobsters a day. They're weighed at the wharf and, after a bit of friendly weather banter, rushed to the kitchen, where bubbling fate awaits. Within hours of emerging from the cold briny deep they're back in local seawater. It's just a bit warmer this time.

FRESH LOCAL SEAWATER

Seawater covers 71 percent of the earth's surface, and 97 percent of that is an average depth of almost four kilometres and an average salinity of 3.5 percent. Maybe that's why all over the world we're drawn to the water's edge in some inexorable way. I make it part of my job. The briny waters surrounding Prince Edward Island are ice covered in the winter, warm in the summer, and teeming with life year-round.

During our brief two-month lobster season we use seawater to properly cook and cool our crustaceans. Every day we gather our share from Back Beach mere minutes away. It's not an easy task. Early in the season that seawater is still frigid, but somebody's got to go to the beach, so off I go.

Properly harvested seawater is not found at the water's edge. The beach is merely what you cross as you enter the water and head offshore to the harvest zone, ignoring whatever surf and crunchy bits you encounter on the way. Extra-long hip waders, a stiff shot of local rum, and a few damn shouts help too.

Here's our expertly honed technique: Choose a beach or shore well away from fuelled boats. Random floaty bits always gather close to shore. Wade out to waist-deep water or so, which is usually much clearer. With a clean bucket and a tight-fitting lid, you're ready. Splash and rinse the bucket once or twice. Dip the bucket completely under the surface of the oncoming current. Smoothly cover it underwater with the lid. It will feel weightless. Return to shore and repeat with any more buckets. With practice you'll find it easy to balance two at once. Back on shore you can trust that the water's natural salinity and impending boil make it eminently safe. Time well spent.

So much of what makes the Inn at Bay Fortune a special place to work or stay is our island home. The flimsiest excuse sends me out the door as I gladly lead our kitchen's foraging efforts. I treasure my time on the land. I don't even mind my time in the icy ocean water.

BAY FORTUNE OYSTERS

The Inn at Bay Fortune is blessed with epically fresh and impeccably briny oysters. When our oyster bar guests ask where our oysters come from, we take great pride in simply saying, "The bay out front, see that buoy?" The next thing we say is, "Slurp all ya like, we're not keeping score!" Fresh, local vegetables are nice, but unlimited oysters from our own sheltered bay are legendary. (Also see photo on page 28.)

We are Oyster Island. The many bays, harbours, rivers, and sheltered coastal waters of Prince Edward Island support one of the world's great oyster fisheries.

Oysters taste of time and place, like chewing the ocean. Uniquely in the world of seafood, they taste very different from bay to bay, from coast to coast. The vigorous shellfish filters 200 litres of water a day, so naturally it tastes like that water, which itself varies wildly. They're often raised in estuaries, where freshwater and seawater blend, and since rainwater flowing to sea carries dissolved minerals in it, the oysters also taste of the nearby land. Prince Edward Island is a red sandbar. There's no rock on our precious isle, only crumbly sandstone, and thus no strong mineral flavours dissolve in our groundwater and find their way to our oysters. Our pure waters allow the natural sweetness of our oysters to shine.

Our ubiquitous Malpeque brand is renowned. The name comes from a specific bay, but any Island oyster can claim the name. Many of our fisherfolk have established their own brands too. They believe in their own hard work, their patch of water, and their oysters. Each is blessed with the wonderful "merroir" of the Island.

Local fisher Dennis McNally apprenticed under the pioneering Flynn brothers of Colville Bay. He set up shop two bays west in Bay Fortune before we relaunched the inn overlooking his valuable lease. None of us knew how big it would get when we began shucking his plump oysters in 2015. Now we serve more than 50,000 a year, most from the bay out front, and Dennis's Red Beard Shellfish Company has become a premium Island brand.

SEA SANDWORT

Foraging wild food is an edible treasure hunt that connects us to Mother Nature's rhythms. Humans have enjoyed this connection since the dawn of time. On Prince Edward Island, we are surrounded by food. Our farmed landscape fabric is legendary. Like so many other places in the world, we're also surrounded by wild food. If you know where and when to look. Sometimes that means you get to see a lot of seals.

The island's many ecosystems contain countless regional plants, many edible, some palatable, a few utterly lip-smacking. Our fields, forests, meadows, hedgerows, stream banks, marshes, and wetlands all offer their own rewards. Even our dunes, sandspits, and beaches are full of edible life. And that's just on shore. Offshore the plant life is equally diverse and delicious.

Sea sandwort is found at the water's edge on the beaches and shores of the North Atlantic, in both North America and Europe. It grows in tightly clustered patches anchored in the sand. The leaves and stems of its tender green stalks are vaguely briny, sweet, and coolly crisp, their flavour hinting at cool cucumber and crisp purslane. They can be eaten raw or lightly steamed. (Also see photo on page 29.)

Many of the wild plants we forage are at their best twice: early in their season, when tender new growth emerges, then much later, once their sweet flowers bloom. In between they toughen as the plant grows and switches from a vegetative to a reproductive state. Sea sandwort stays edible all summer long, though, its texture crisp and tender. The plant's heartiness helps it survive a harsh environment.

Most local beaches have sea sandwort patches here and there, but at the inn we prefer the dense hedges of Seal Beach. It's close by but adventurous, with a bumpy dirt road, a farmer's field, perilous steps cut into a steep bank, and a long beach stroll ahead. Ninety percent of our time is spent just getting there and back. But why would we rush a long beach walk? Upon arrival we enjoy the easy harvest and spending time with the ever-present pod of seals just across the narrow channel.

SPRUCE TIPS

Spruce tips, like so many other foraged crops, are among the first growth of spring. The annual rhythm of foraging season always begins with a flurry of spring action as many wild plants emerge from the warming soil. Most are fresh vegetables to us, to be eaten the day they're picked. Spruce tips are the rosemary of Prince Edward Island. Their intense resinous fragrance is distinctive yet familiar. The beautiful flavour of the tender young needles and their brief season inspire countless uses and preservation methods in the FireWorks kitchen.

In June each year the spruce tree hedgerows lining the farmed fields of the island come alive. After a winter of dormancy, the trees' spring growth emerges as tiny purple pods at the tip of every little branch from the previous year. In their first few days the needles are light green, tender, and fragrant. In mere weeks the summer sun hardens them into the dark green mature growth that defines the tree, and the needles toughen to the point of bitterness. However, harvested at just the right time, the new growth, the spruce tips, are delicious, vaguely sweet, barely bitter and comfortably aromatic like a Christmas tree.

Firs, pines, and cedars are similar softwoods with tender, edible young tips. Later in the summer they all produce intensely fragrant flower pollen. Rare and potent with a distinctive woodsy aroma. Worth climbing trees for because these flower pockets don't appear on every branch or even every tree. With careful vigilance we'll spot them, sometimes higher up the tree than the easily accessible spruce tips at the base.

Like rosemary, spruce tips are minced, chopped, ground into salt or sugar, infused into syrups, steeped in alcohol, or thrust into the lead aromatic role in a variety of savoury and sweet dishes.

NASTURTIUM FLOWERS
AND LEAVES

Nasturtiums are the first seeds we plant every year. We sow in long rows of hanging baskets in our greenhouses, anticipating the cascading plants. They're not destined for our flower vases, though. On our culinary farm, everything finds its way to the kitchen.

Nasturtiums are natives of Central and South America that made their way to Europe before they came to North America. Along the way they were sometimes food, sometimes ornamental. On Prince Edward Island they're a favourite in flower beds and hanging baskets. Thirty years ago, their delicious leaves and flowers found their way into my legendary salad bowl at the Inn at Bay Fortune and they have been a staple ever since.

Nasturtiums have a beautiful fresh green herbaceous flavour and a sharp, peppery edge similar to arugula, radish, and watercress. Like many plants, their flowers are also noticeably sweet, making them a signature ingredient in our nightly salad. Few ingredients are as aromatic, colourful, sweet, and snappy.

Nasturtiums thrive in poor soil yet are somehow intensely nutritious. They're a favourite of bees, so we plant them everywhere to encourage pollination of the surrounding plants.

The nasturtiums we grow in our greenhouses are tended solely for their flowers. We start them as early as possible so they'll be ready for our annual late-May opening. We leave their leaves alone, so they'll produce flowers prolifically all summer long. From our many outside beds we harvest the whole plant—flowers, leaves large and small, tender stems, and later in the season, the seed pods left by falling flowers. We pickle these tiny, tender pods like capers.

GIN ROSES

The dirt roads and back corners of Prince Edward Island are full of forgotten rose bushes, long left to bloom alone. Where farmhouses once stood, this hearty plant remains, overgrown into thick patches of tall, thorny bushes. Their annual riot of colour is usually enjoyed from a distance, their wild fragrance borne on the breeze to tempt every bee within miles. But some rose bushes are worth wading into.

Thousands of rose varieties have been cultivated for thousands of years in thousands of places. The plant is ubiquitous. A rainbow of colours and a range of fragrances are found around the globe. Depending on your perspective, each variety offers its own advantages. But if you're intent on soaking a case of gin, only one bush in one place will do. And I'm not telling where it is.

Most roses are grown for ornamental enjoyment, but they also have culinary uses. Fragrant petals easily infuse their flavour and colour into cream, water, and alcohol. Rosehips, the plant's late-season fruit, are rich in flavour too. But not every rose bush is the same. Some taste simply bland or turn our gin a murky drab colour. Over time we've found that one particular bush offers the best flavour and brightest colour.

Foraging requires patience. You have to know the right moment to harvest. After a winter of waiting, it's easy to jump the gun, but pick too early and quality and yield suffer. When the flower is still tightly closed or just opening, it's easy to pick, but its fragrance is still building. When the flower fully forms, it reaches peak perfume, and there's just a day or so to pick before the petals fall away and the bees fly away.

Foraging semi-wild rose petals can hurt. Bees sting. They're also wildly distracted by the same flowers you are. Arm yourself with long sleeves, a gardener's mesh hat, and most important, thin disposable gloves for your fingers. To harvest, tap each flower to warn off any hidden occupants, then surround the petals with your fingers and pull from the base. Mature fragrant flowers release easily. Occasionally you'll encounter an angry bee, but your gloves will protect you. Try not to accumulate any little green leaves, as they're bitter.

RADISH PODS

The humble radish is one of the simplest yet most profound plants we grow. It's so easy to sprout that it's a classroom staple and science fair regular. It's also a prime example of one of our core farming tenets: life cycle harvesting.

We established our farm to grow vegetables, soil, and knowledge. Over the years we've learned so much by just eliminating the middleperson. Our kitchen and farm are connected. We don't just see vegetables in a box—we see plants in the soil. We nurture plants from seed to sprout to harvest and back to seed again. Naturally we find inspiration every step of the way.

We found a forgotten radish patch a few years back, a radish crop seemingly past its prime. We had a second season of peppery flower foraging. A random discovery of a tender seed pod. We're far from the first to discover the full potential of this plant, but when we did it inspired a revolutionary new way of looking at our farm that endures.

In five days, a radish seed sprouts into a mildly snappy cotyledon, the plant's very first green growth. This microgreen is one of our favourite garnishes. In twenty days, we pluck a marble-sized radish with its long tail intact below and first tender green shoots above. At thirty days we harvest a classic radish and its full greens. We have until day forty-five or so before the root toughens, but we keep picking the leaves. After sixty days the plant shifts from its vegetative state to the reproductive state and the leaves become bitter. It also begins inexhaustibly producing tasty flowers. At ninety days we pick tender green seed pods that rank among the most delicious vegetables we grow—sweet and crispy like a snap pea but peppery like a radish. By 120 days the pods have matured and toughened and we're back to seeds. With sequential planting, radishes and their full life cycle are a part of our culinary farm all season long.

Radish seed pods are tender yet crisp, sweet, juicy, green, and fresh. Best of all, they taste just like radishes—as do all the other crops we harvest from the humble radish.

LOVAGE POLLEN

Lovage has long been my favourite herb. I planted it thirty years ago in my first herb garden and I've loved it ever since. Its bright green celery-like flavour is familiar yet distinctive. It's an edible grace note, adding intensity to other flavours. Unlike most other herbs, cooked lovage retains its bright green colour. It's also the tallest herb on our farm by far, easily topping a six-foot chef. I concede. I love lovage. (Also see photo on page 42.)

After a seven-year lovage affair I moved on from the inn but spent seventeen years sneaking back into the garden for my favourite flavour. When my wife, Chazz, and I relaunched the property, we immediately established a proper farm and naturally planted lots of my favourite herb. The lovage hedge became a reliable source for early-season fresh flavour, but would inevitably bolt over my head into bitterness.

One late-summer afternoon I wandered by the lovage patch newly armed with our farm's life cycle harvesting perspective. I had never really noticed the plant's delicate flowers before, but I did that day. Though some were brown and dried, most were young and bright, and many seemed to glisten in the afternoon light.

I immediately crammed some of the sticky lovage flower pollen into my mouth. It was impossibly delicious. Fragrant beyond the flavour I knew so well, with none of the normal bitterness and an unfamiliar sweetness. It was as if every bit of the plant had gone into reaching for the sky, thrusting this fragrant flower as far as possible towards the sun. It was a revelation, and it had been right in front of me for thirty years.

Our culinary farm was founded to see what would happen when we blurred the lines between a farm and a kitchen. What we've found is inspiring. Among many beautiful lessons, a flower pollen revelation remains powerfully validating and a reminder that if you try, you really can learn something new every day.

WHOLE-GRAIN CHALLENGES

Real bread is baked with love and served with symbolism, every loaf tells the story of its provenance so our dedication to Prince Edward Island inspires us to bake bread with grain exclusively grown by local farmers. (Also see photo on page 43.) We break it nightly to begin our feast and treasure sharing its natural fermentation, wood-oven baking, and Island-grown provenance. It's not always easy to support the food system around us, though.

The economics of our modern global food system can make it challenging to find things in our own backyard. Once upon a time, market-garden family farms dotted the North American landscape, but today large monoculture farms dominate. The global choices available to consumers have squeezed out local diversity. Island farmers smartly focus on potatoes, while out West, grain reigns supreme.

We don't need modern highly engineered, high-gluten flour to bake bread. We make our dough with various heritage grains grown on the island long ago by Acadian settlers and nurtured today by a handful of local organic farmers. We love the rich flavour of Red Fife in particular, the grain our settlers planted as they broke virgin prairie sod. These real whole grains don't produce cloud-like modern white bread, but nor do they bake doorstops.

We've learned with care and attention to bake and proudly serve rustic, real bread nightly. We've mastered our local flour's lower gluten content and learned to coax it to tenderness with natural fermentation. We could have easily given up and baked with a measure of strengthening white flour, but we don't. We say our flour is from the Island, and it is. We bake hard work and respect for our local farmers into every loaf. Our guests love our bread, and we love that it shows our devotion to our mission.

OUR HERB HOUSE

On our culinary farm perhaps no place is as special to us as our herb house. Within its warm embrace, we've created an essential microclimate, both practical and experimental, by merely enclosing the space, insulating it from the wind, and capturing the sun's warmth in the soil. Our kitchen needs a reliable source of fresh herbs, so the environment is designed to give us an annual jump-start of early-season essential flavours before our outdoor farm and herb gardens come online.

In the summer, the herb house is a place of intense life and flavour. A roster of culinary herbs and equally vibrant wild weeds thrive inside where it's warmer sooner and stays hotter all season long. They're stronger and heartier, and they burst to life ahead of the plants outside. In winter the pace slows down. Within the insulated space the herbs lie dormant, but the earth in our raised beds never freezes. Outside, our zone 5 farm and gardens may be frozen stiff, but within, a bit of warmer zone 6 thrives. We even create our own little corner of zone 7 Mediterranean every winter by building a digitally heated smaller greenhouse-within-a-greenhouse, insulating our particularly vulnerable rosemary and lemon verbena. In our herb house we grow Kentucky Colonel spearmint, chocolate mint, lemon and English thyme, French tarragon, purple and common sage, lavender, anise hyssop, golden and classic oregano, garlic and chives, summer savory, and bronze and green fennel.

The permanent perennial plantings in our herb house benefit from a gentler annual life cycle. Overwintering makes them better producers. With observant life cycle harvesting, we harvest fresh leaves and eventually flowers from the herbs. We wait patiently for our fennel plants to produce delicious yellow flowers, and we wait even longer for their brightly flavoured fresh green seeds. We harvest them before they harden into the familiar shelf-stable spice. Their subtle sweet fragrance is an epic annual treat that validates every drop of effort we put into the herb house.

HAPPY PIGS

Today's food system gives consumers extreme convenience and broad choices at historically inexpensive prices. It's a spectacular success when you consider that our planet is better fed at less cost to us than ever before. This all comes with many hidden costs, though, including all the distance from death we demand.

Since recorded history, humans have craved meat, although for most of that time we consumed very little—it was a seasonal treat at best. Many of the world's cuisines still treat meat as a scarce resource, as a condiment rather than a main attraction. Today our collective craving drives an enormous industry that has single-handedly changed more of our environment than any other, including oil, gas, and transportation. Our dinner plate choices have profound impacts on the world around us. Especially when we ignore where what we eat came from.

Historically, vegetarians eschewed meat because their diets were founded on the principle of nonviolence towards animals. In modern times, they eschew the less than ideal conditions animals are subjected to on our behalf when we demand cheaply priced industrially raised meat. In the FireWorks kitchen we share those values thus prefer to work with farmers that raise their livestock humanely. We remain troubled, though, by our planet's over-consumption of meat, by how much that has changed our climate, and by the consumer ignorance that facilitates it.

Every year three piglets join us for a season of sun basking, earth wallowing, and plant-based dining. They're quickly adopted by our cooks and given the best of our kitchen scraps. We treat them as vegetarians, since it's better for their omnivorous systems. They're the happiest pigs on Prince Edward Island. They live a good life. They just have one bad day.

When our pigs die two things happen. We miss them, and thus we respect them. Our love for them as sentient beings validates our own humanity. As cooks we do our very best through our art and craft to show that respect. It's a profound lesson, but as humans we need to go further. We have an ethical responsibility to consume less meat, and all of it must be sustainably produced. Just like our happy pigs.

OUR LOCAL SUPPLIERS

Running a restaurant and country inn, we're fortunate to be in the business of making friends. It's a gracious way to spend a life.

Before we welcome new friends, though, every day our old friends give us strength. Like any great food destination, we're an authentic reflection of our surroundings. We farm and strive to do so much for ourselves, but we would not be what we are without the equally passionate food artisans of Prince Edward Island. They too are inspired by our island home, and we're proud to share their hard work with our guests.

Jeff McCourt of Glasgow Glen Farm is a born-again chef. After a distinguished culinary career that included five glorious years as my sous-chef at the inn in the 1990s, a few years at the helm after I left, and various other posts near and far, Jeff saw the light and retired. He became a dad and a cheesemaker. He knows that he's fortunate to craft cheese from some of the richest dairy on the planet.

I've known Jeff a long time. He epitomizes the many and varied passionate culinary artisans of the Island. He's rooted in our red earth, fiercely tenacious, and quietly creative, and he has worked harder than anyone I know to make his business a success. Somehow throughout it all he always finds the time to volunteer in a charity kitchen or coach a sports team. He's a true family man. I look up to him. We know his story. We respect his cheese. He proudly represents so many others.

Of the many, many lessons Prince Edward Island has taught me, none has so powerfully defined my cooking style as my fortunate connection to the hard work behind real ingredients. When we see beyond the freshness of the ingredient to the story of human beings like Jeff, it pushes us to do our best as cooks, to love our shared ingredients the way they were loved by their creators.

I'm convinced that our guests taste that love too.

Country Inn
Breakfast

IRON TRIO

GOOD MORNING SMOOTHIE,
COUNTRY INN GRANOLA PARFAIT, FRESH FRUIT JUICE

This trio of simple flavours is a five-star start to our guests' day. As they sit for breakfast each morning, we always greet them with light, bright flavours. We feel the first taste of the day should be nutritious *and* delicious, so we patiently make our own yogurt, craft our own whole-grain granola, preserve exclusively local fruit all season, blend an all-natural, nutrient-dense macrobiotic smoothie, fresh-press orange juice, and even pick dew-covered fresh mint at the break of dawn. We also offer the indulgences of a full-blown North American breakfast with our own impeccable farm-fresh ingredients, but we still begin with our healthy best. To round out your trio, add your favourite fruit juice. We often include orange juice or, during the season, locally pressed cider.

Good Morning Smoothie

We make the same smoothie for our guests that I do for my kids. No added sugar or artificial additives, of course—just lots of nutritional real fruit and the probiotic yogurt that unites the works.

———————————

Toss everything into a high-speed blender and process until silky and smooth, about 1 minute.

Serves 2 to 4, makes about 4 cups (1 L)

2 ripe bananas
2 cups (500 mL) frozen blueberries or other frozen fruit
1 cup (250 mL) freshly squeezed Valencia orange juice or locally pressed cider (avoid bitter navel oranges)
1 cup (250 mL) natural plain full-fat yogurt
A large handful of fresh mint leaves

recipe continues

Country Inn Granola Parfait

This gold-standard granola has always been our family's favourite, so it's only natural we share it with our country inn guests and your home too. It's packed with more than enough whole-grain goodness to start everyone's day. The granola's ingredients are flexible too. Maintain the basic volume measures within the nut-and-seed category but feel free to simplify or improvise, substituting your favourite ingredients. We do with every batch. We stick to the formula, but since we make granola almost daily we constantly try different ingredient combinations. This recipe makes a big batch of granola, so you'll have plenty on hand for several breakfasts.

Our tangy homemade yogurt shines in this parfait, but any natural plain full-fat yogurt will give you equally delicious results. The whole-grain granola topping is crunchy, while the fruit preserve on the bottom is an unexpected yet balanced treat.

Make the Country Inn Granola
Preheat the oven to 325°F (160°C). Line 2 baking sheets with parchment paper or foil and lightly oil.

Measure the vegetable oil into a small saucepan. Use the same measuring cup for the honey to ease the sticky mess. Add the honey to the oil along with the cinnamon, nutmeg, and vanilla. Whisk over medium heat until the honey smoothly melts into the oil, a minute or two.

Toss the oats into a large bowl, pour in the spiced honey, and stir until thoroughly combined. Divide the oat mixture evenly between the prepared baking sheets. Bake, stirring every 10 minutes, until golden brown and fragrant, 45 minutes or so.

Meanwhile, in the same bowl, toss together the pine nuts, pistachios, walnuts, sunflower seeds, pumpkin seeds, flaxseeds, and raisins.

Carefully scrape the hot granola into the bowl. Toss everything together while the granola is still hot, then let cool. Transfer to an airtight container or resealable plastic bag and store at room temperature for up to 2 weeks.

Make the Parfait
Divide the strawberry citrus stew among 4 wide-mouth 1-cup (250 mL) mason jars. Carefully add a thick layer of yogurt. Top with country inn granola. Serve immediately or cover tightly and refrigerate overnight.

Makes 4 parfaits, about 15 cups (3.4 L) granola

COUNTRY INN GRANOLA
1 cup (250 mL) vegetable oil
1 cup (250 mL) pure liquid honey
1 tablespoon (15 mL) cinnamon
1 tablespoon (15 mL) nutmeg
1 tablespoon (15 mL) pure vanilla extract
8 cups (2 L) quick-cooking or large-flake oats
1 cup (250 mL) toasted pine nuts
1 cup (250 mL) unsalted roasted pistachios
1 cup (250 mL) toasted walnut halves
1 cup (250 mL) unsalted roasted sunflower seeds
1 cup (250 mL) unsalted roasted pumpkin seeds
1 cup (250 mL) flaxseeds, lightly ground
2 cups (500 mL) raisins, prunes, or other dried fruits

PARFAIT
1 cup (250 mL) Strawberry Citrus Stew (page 251) or your favourite preserved fruit
1½ cups (375 mL) natural plain full-fat yogurt
1½ cups (375 mL) Country Inn Granola or your favourite all-natural granola or muesli

NUTMEG BREAKFAST BAKES

BLUEBERRY STEW, LEMON VERBENA CURD

Extravagance and luxury—that's what we do at the inn, and it starts first thing in the morning. Blurring the lines between last night's dessert and this morning's breakfast, this dish is for luxuriously sleeping in and enjoying leisurely room service from an unseen kitchen and unknown dishwasher. At home, though, someone is going to have to stay up late or get up first. No worries. This sort of bright karma first thing in the morning is guaranteed to set the cook up for a day of earthly rewards.

Blueberry Stew

Wild blueberries are sweetened with maple syrup and brightened with lemon. Vanilla balances the fruit's flavour, while the cornstarch thickens the juices.

2 cups (500 mL) fresh or frozen wild blueberries
½ cup (125 mL) pure maple syrup
Zest of 1 lemon
Juice of ½ lemon
¼ teaspoon (1 mL) pure vanilla extract
1 tablespoon (15 mL) cornstarch

In a small saucepan, combine the blueberries, maple syrup, lemon zest and juice, vanilla, and cornstarch. Stir gently over medium-high heat for a few minutes, until the mixture simmers and thickens. Remove from the heat and reserve until needed. Serve warm.

Serves 4 to 6

PREP AND PLAN
- Make the Blueberry Stew and Lemon Verbena Curd up to 1 day in advance.
- Make and bake the Nutmeg Breakfast Bakes just before serving.

recipe continues

Lemon Verbena Curd

Lemon curd tastes like thick lemonade. It's the perfect smear of tangy, bright flavour to balance the sweet blueberries.

½ cup (125 mL) sugar
12 fresh lemon verbena leaves (or leaves from
    6 sprigs fresh thyme or 4 sprigs fresh rosemary)
Zest and juice of 3 lemons
4 egg yolks
1 teaspoon (5 mL) pure vanilla extract
6 tablespoons (90 mL) butter, softened

Measure the sugar, herb leaves, and lemon zest into a food processor, using a small bowl attachment if you have one. Process, scraping down the sides once or twice, until finely minced and fragrant. Transfer to a medium saucepan along with the lemon juice, egg yolks, vanilla, and butter. Stir continuously over medium heat as a beautiful sauce smooths and thickens, 5 minutes or so. Do not let it boil. Transfer to a storage container. Use immediately or tightly seal and refrigerate until breakfast.

Nutmeg Breakfast Bakes

The ratio of eggs, milk, and flour in this batter makes it soufflé into a light, tender pastry. It's a particularly tasty way to show off nutmeg's perfume, but feel free to try other spices such as cinnamon or cardamom.

1 cup (250 mL) whole milk
4 eggs
1 cup (250 mL) all-purpose flour
2 tablespoons (30 mL) sugar
1 teaspoon (5 mL) freshly grated nutmeg
1 teaspoon (5 mL) pure vanilla extract
¼ teaspoon (1 mL) salt
Zest of 1 orange

Preheat the oven to 425°F (220°C). Turn on the convection fan if you have one. Place six 6-inch (15 cm) lightly oiled cast-iron skillets in the oven. (Alternatively, you can use six 8-ounce/250 mL ramekins placed on a baking sheet.)

In a high-speed blender or food processor, combine the milk, eggs, flour, sugar, nutmeg, vanilla, salt, and orange zest. Process until thoroughly combined. Carefully divide the batter among the preheated moulds. Bake until golden brown and puffed, about 20 minutes. Rest for a few minutes before serving.

PLATE AND PRESENTATION
- Top with a dollop of Lemon Verbena Curd.
- Add a heaping spoonful of the Blueberry Stew on top of the Nutmeg Breakfast Bakes.

COUNTRY INN PANCAKES

BUMBLEBERRY COMPOTE

For many guests, an extravagant breakfast is their favourite part of our country inn experience, so memorable pancakes are an essential part of our repertoire. Our guests love their sizzling arrival in individual cast-iron skillets. These pancakes deliver the perfect balance of hearty whole-grain goodness in a light, fluffy batter. They're a year-round favourite in my house, but at the inn they're particularly excellent during the summer, when our various berry seasons overlap into a multi-berry compote topping traditionally known as bumbleberry. You can substitute frozen berries any time of year. Once thawed, the berries are softer and juicier but, with impeccable provenance, can sometimes be more delicious than come-from-away fresh.

Make the Bumbleberry Compote

In a medium saucepan, combine the blueberries, maple syrup, lemon zest and juice, and vanilla. Bring to a full simmer over medium heat, stirring gently. Remove from the heat. Stir in the strawberries, then to preserve their shape, gently fold in the raspberries and blackberries. Rest for at least an hour, allowing the juices and flavours to deliciously mingle and form a compote, or cover and refrigerate for up to a week.

Make the Country Inn Pancakes

Preheat a large skillet or griddle over medium heat.

In a large bowl, whisk together the all-purpose flour, whole wheat flour, oats, baking powder, nutmeg, and salt, evenly distributing the finer powders amidst the coarser ones.

In a medium bowl and using the same whisk, whisk together the eggs, milk, and vanilla. Pour the wet ingredients into the dry. Switch to a wooden spoon and thoroughly stir the batter until smooth.

Lightly coat the skillet with a splash of vegetable oil. Spoon in the batter, making pancakes the size and shape you prefer. Cook until the bottom is golden brown. Flip carefully and continue cooking until lightly browned on the bottom and fully cooked. Serve with the bumbleberry compote or your favourite topping.

Serves 6 to 8

BUMBLEBERRY COMPOTE
1 cup (250 mL) fresh or frozen blueberries
1 cup (250 mL) pure maple syrup
Zest and juice of 1 lemon
1 teaspoon (5 mL) pure vanilla extract
1 cup (250 mL) fresh strawberries, hulled and quartered
1 cup (250 mL) fresh raspberries
1 cup (250 mL) fresh blackberries

COUNTRY INN PANCAKES
1 cup (250 mL) all-purpose flour
1 cup (250 mL) whole wheat flour
1 cup (250 mL) quick-cooking oats
2 tablespoons (30 mL) baking powder
1 teaspoon (5 mL) nutmeg
½ teaspoon (2 mL) sea salt
4 eggs
2 cups (500 mL) whole milk
1 tablespoon (15 mL) pure vanilla extract
Vegetable oil or melted butter, for frying

OATMEAL-CRUSTED FRENCH TOAST

APPLE RUM BUTTER

This is five-star French toast. Chewy brioche patiently soaked in exotically spiced creamy custard, crusted with crunchy oats, lightly browned in butter, then topped with intensely concentrated apple butter from last year's harvest. It's as extravagantly delicious as we can make it. If you don't have Apple Rum Butter, this is just as good served with your favourite fruit compote or good old-fashioned maple syrup.

Preheat a large, heavy skillet or griddle over medium-low heat.

Crack the eggs into a large bowl. Whisk in the milk, maple syrup, vanilla, and cardamom.

Arrange the bread slices in a single layer in a large shallow baking dish. Pour the egg mixture over the bread. Rest, turning once or twice, until most of the egg mixture is absorbed, about 5 minutes. Pour the oats into a shallow dish or plate.

Pour 1 tablespoon (15 mL) of the vegetable oil into the hot pan. Add 2 tablespoons (30 mL) of the butter to the oil. Swirl until sizzling, adding the butter flavour without burning it. Working with as many slices of bread as will fit in your pan, dredge the slices, one at a time, in the oats, turning to evenly coat each side and pressing gently to ensure the oats adhere. Transfer to the hot pan, adjusting the heat to keep the pan gently sizzling. Cook until the bottoms are golden brown and crisp, 3 or 4 minutes. Flip carefully and continue to cook until the second side is golden brown, 2 or 3 minutes more. (You can place the first few slices in a warm oven for a few minutes while you finish up.) Repeat to cook the remaining bread slices, adding more oil and butter as needed. Serve with lots of apple rum butter.

Serves 4

4 eggs
1 cup (250 mL) whole milk
¼ cup (60 mL) pure maple syrup, more for serving if needed
1 tablespoon (15 mL) pure vanilla extract
1 teaspoon (5 mL) ground cardamom, nutmeg, or cinnamon
8 thick slices of brioche or your favourite bread
1 cup (250 mL) quick-cooking or large-flake oats
2 tablespoons (30 mL) vegetable oil, divided, for frying
4 tablespoons (60 mL) butter, divided, for frying
Apple Rum Butter (page 248), for serving

SMOKED SALMON POTATO CAKES

LOBSTER HOLLANDAISE

This is our extravagant local version of classic eggs Benedict. Our version is built on crispy-crusted tender potato cakes loaded with our own smoked salmon. Crisp artisanal bacon and a perfectly oozing poached egg topped with decadently rich lobster hollandaise sauce completes the presentation.

Best of all, that pure lobster flavour is free. Lobster shells left over from dinner are still packed with flavour. We break up the shells and slowly bake them in melted butter to create intensely flavoured lobster-infused butter that we then use to make this hollandaise. We even re-infuse the same butter several times to intensify the flavour. It's time-consuming business but worth it. We serve lots of guests, generate lots of lobster shells, and extract lots of flavour from them.

Smoked Salmon Potato Cakes

These potato cakes are loaded with smoked salmon, deliciously tender on the inside and delightfully crispy on the outside.

4 tablespoons (60 mL) butter, divided, for frying
2 yellow onions, thinly sliced
2 garlic cloves, finely minced
2 large russet potatoes (about 1 pound/450 g), unpeeled and thinly sliced
2 tablespoons (30 mL) finely minced fresh thyme
Salt and pepper
¼ cup (60 mL) dry white wine
½ cup (125 mL) heavy (35%) cream
¾ pound (340 g) smoked salmon slices
1 cup (250 mL) all-purpose flour
4 eggs, vigorously whisked
2 cups (500 mL) panko crumbs
Vegetable oil, for frying

Preheat the oven to 350°F (180°C). Turn on the convection fan if you have one.

recipe continues

Serves 6

PREP AND PLAN
- Make the Lobster Butter (page 249) 2 or 3 days in advance. You'll use it in the Lobster Hollandaise.
- Make and shape (but don't coat or fry) the Smoked Salmon Potato Cakes 1 or 2 days in advance.
- When it's time for breakfast, crisp 12 bacon strips, make the Lobster Hollandaise, fry the potato cakes, then poach 6 eggs.

Melt 2 tablespoons (30 mL) of the butter in a large saucepan or skillet over medium-high heat. Toss in the onions and garlic and sauté, stirring frequently without browning, until sizzling hot and fragrant, 10 minutes or so. Add the potatoes and thyme and season with salt and pepper. Stir until evenly combined. Pour in the white wine and cream and bring the mixture to a full simmer. Gently stir in the salmon; it will break into smaller pieces. Transfer the filling to a 13 x 9-inch (3.5 L) baking pan or dish. Smooth the surface with the back of a spatula or spoon. Bake until the potatoes are tender and have absorbed the surrounding liquid, about 30 minutes.

Evenly press the potatoes with a spatula to level their surface. Cover and refrigerate until thoroughly cold and firm, at least 8 hours or overnight.

Using a large biscuit cutter, cut out 6 potato cakes. Remove with your fingers and gently form into evenly shaped cakes about 1 inch (2.5 cm) thick. Arrange on a large plate and refrigerate or freeze until firm enough to hold together, 15 minutes or so.

Place the flour, eggs, and panko in 3 separate shallow bowls. To minimize the mess of breaded fingers, use one hand exclusively to handle the potato cakes while they are dry with flour or panko and the other while they are wet with egg. Working with one potato cake at a time, gently dredge in the flour, dusting off excess flour. Thoroughly dip through the eggs, draining off excess egg. Lastly, give them a roll through the panko.

Heat a large non-stick skillet over medium heat. Pour in a splash of vegetable oil and add the remaining 2 tablespoons (30 mL) butter. Add the potato cakes and slowly, patiently brown them. Keep the pan sizzling gently and turn the cakes occasionally until they are evenly crisped and thoroughly cooked, about 15 minutes in total. Keep the finished cakes in a warm oven for a few minutes until ready to serve.

Lobster Hollandaise

This classic sauce is luxuriously flavoured with rich lobster-scented butter.

4 egg yolks
Zest and juice of 1 lemon
2 tablespoons (30 mL) dry white wine or cold water
1 or 2 dashes of hot sauce
⅔ cup (150 mL) Lobster Butter (page 249), clarified butter, or brown butter, melted and warm but not too hot for your finger

In a medium saucepan, bring an inch or so of water to a simmer. In a large metal bowl, whisk together the egg yolks, lemon zest and juice, white wine, and hot sauce until light and frothy. Place the bowl directly over the simmering water and continue whisking until the mixture thickens, 3 or 4 minutes. Remove the bowl from the heat and, whisking constantly, slowly drizzle in the warm lobster butter. Continue whisking until the sauce thickens, 2 or 3 minutes. Serve immediately or cover tightly and rest over the pot of hot water, off the heat, for up to 30 minutes.

PLATE AND PRESENTATION

A few sprigs fresh thyme, basil, mint, or other herb and edible flowers

- Crisscross 2 crisp bacon strips on a plate.
- Position a Smoked Salmon Potato Cake over the bacon.
- Top with a poached egg (or prepared as desired).
- Drench with lots of Lobster Hollandaise.
- Garnish with the fresh herbs and edible flowers.

EXTRA-CINNAMON ROLLS

Our cinnamon rolls are legendary for their sweet, tender dough infused with brown butter and filled with buttery brown sugar and the very best aromatic cinnamon on the globe. We prefer intensely aromatic Ceylon or fiery Vietnamese cinnamon over mainstream cassia. These cinnamon rolls bring guests back year after year begging for more. Some guests even resort to outright thievery and primal hoarding. We understand. Our staff can't resist them either, so we bake enough every day for them too. Even our couriers and technicians know they can count on a treat when they make a delivery or service call. Maybe that's why we're always first on the route.

We bake individual large cinnamon rolls in miniature iron skillets for our guests, but in this recipe you simply nestle them together in a larger pan.

Make the Sweet Dough

Set up a stand mixer fitted with the dough hook.

Toss the butter into a medium saucepan over medium-high heat. Swirl gently as it melts, foams, and eventually lightly browns. Transfer to the stand mixer. Pour the milk into the saucepan and stir over medium-high heat until steamy hot but not quite simmering. Stir in the brown sugar and vanilla, then add to the brown butter. Evenly sprinkle the yeast over the top. Rest for a minute or two as the yeast dissolves. Add 4 cups (1 L) of the flour and knead on low speed until a sticky yet smooth dough forms, about 10 minutes. Cover the bowl with a kitchen towel and rest the dough until it rises, about 1 hour.

Meanwhile, in a small bowl, whisk together the remaining ½ cup (125 mL) flour, baking powder, baking soda, and salt. Knead the mixture into the risen dough until evenly combined. Cover tightly with plastic wrap and refrigerate for an hour to help relax its elasticity. It will rise slightly.

Preheat the oven to 350°F (180°C). Turn on the convection fan if you have one. Lightly oil a 12-inch (30 cm) non-stick skillet or baking pan.

recipe continues

Makes 12 rolls

SWEET DOUGH
8 tablespoons (125 mL) butter
2 cups (500 mL) whole milk
½ cup (125 mL) tightly packed brown sugar
1 teaspoon (5 mL) pure vanilla extract
1 packet (¼ ounce/7 g) active dry yeast (2 heaping teaspoons/12 mL)
4½ cups (1.125 L) all-purpose flour, divided
½ teaspoon (2 mL) baking powder
½ teaspoon (2 mL) baking soda
½ teaspoon (2 mL) sea salt

CINNAMON FILLING
8 tablespoons (125 mL) butter, melted and cooled to room temperature
1 teaspoon (5 mL) pure vanilla extract
¼ cup (60 mL) white sugar
¼ cup (60 mL) tightly packed brown sugar
2 tablespoons (30 mL) cinnamon

CINNAMON ICING
1 cup (250 mL) icing sugar
1 tablespoon (15 mL) cinnamon
2 teaspoons (10 mL) lemon juice
1 teaspoon (5 mL) pure vanilla extract

Lightly flour a work surface, your hands, and a rolling pin. Transfer the risen dough to the floured surface and sprinkle with a little more flour. Roll out into a 10 x 20-inch (25 x 50 cm) rectangle with a long side facing you, flipping once or twice and using more flour if needed to keep it from sticking. Brush as much flour off the dough as you can.

Make the Cinnamon Filling and Bake the Cinnamon Rolls

In a small bowl, stir together the melted butter and vanilla. Brush evenly over the dough, going right to the edges. In a separate small bowl, whisk together the white sugar, brown sugar, and cinnamon. Sprinkle evenly over the buttered dough.

Starting at the long end, roll up the dough as tightly as you can, forming a thick, even log. Pinch the seam to seal it. Cut the log into 12 even slices. Carefully fit the slices, cut side up, into the oiled skillet. Bake until golden brown and risen, about 40 minutes. Remove and rest for a few minutes until cool enough to handle.

Make the Cinnamon Icing

Meanwhile, in a small bowl, whisk together the icing sugar, cinnamon, lemon juice, and vanilla. Drizzle over the slightly cooled cinnamon rolls. For a more festive look, transfer the icing to a small resealable plastic bag. Snip off a corner of the bag and squeeze the icing decoratively over the buns. Enjoy immediately or store tightly sealed at room temperature for up to 2 days.

BLUEBERRY BROWN BUTTER MUFFINS

On Prince Edward Island thousands of acres are devoted to wild blueberry fields. They're a high-value crop that have a long tradition of popping up in muffins. Our favourite blueberry muffins are loaded with fruit and every bit of extra flavour our bakers can cram into them—rich moistness from brown butter and tangy yogurt, exotic yet comforting cardamom, so much buttery streusel topping you can't see the rest of the muffin, and lots of intensely flavoured local wild blueberries. Even a blueberry muffin can be extravagant.

Make the Muffin Batter

Preheat the oven to 350°F (180°C). Turn on the convection fan if you have one. Lightly oil 12 muffin cups with cooking spray or line with paper liners.

Toss the butter into a small saucepan over medium-high heat. Swirl gently as it melts, foams, and eventually lightly browns. Remove from the heat.

In a large bowl, whisk together the flour, sugar, cardamom, baking powder, and salt.

In another large bowl, whisk together the eggs, vanilla, and lemon zest. Whisk in the yogurt until smooth. Pour in the brown butter, taking care to scrape in every last drop of flavourful brown sediment. Stir to combine. Add about two-thirds of the flour mixture. Switch to a rubber spatula or wooden spoon and stir until the batter is smooth. Stir in the remaining flour mixture. Barely stir in the blueberries with just a few last vigorous strokes. Evenly portion the batter into the muffin cups.

Make the Streusel Topping and Bake the Muffins

In a small bowl, whisk together the sugar and flour. Add the butter and rub in with your fingers until thoroughly crumbly. Sprinkle evenly over the muffin batter. Bake until golden brown, about 30 minutes. Enjoy immediately or store tightly sealed at room temperature for up to 2 days.

Makes 12 muffins

MUFFIN BATTER
10 tablespoons (150 mL) butter
2½ cups (625 mL) all-purpose flour
¾ cup (175 mL) sugar
1 tablespoon (15 mL) ground cardamom
1 tablespoon (15 mL) baking powder
½ teaspoon (5 mL) salt
3 eggs
1 tablespoon (15 mL) pure vanilla extract
Zest of 2 lemons
1 cup (250 mL) natural plain full-fat yogurt
2 cups (500 mL) fresh or frozen blueberries

STREUSEL TOPPING
½ cup (125 mL) sugar
¼ cup (60 mL) all-purpose flour
4 tablespoons (60 mL) cold butter

The Fire Garden

WILD ROSE COCKTAILS

ROSE NEGRONI, ROSE GIN FIZZ

Before the feast begins, our guests love to wander our whimsical grounds with one of our signature cocktails in hand. We craft these with locally distilled gin and a deliciously fragrant twist of hand-picked wild roses (see page 36) from a secret rose bush that I personally forage on my ongoing wild-harvest rounds. I steep the petals in my family doctor's gin until their lush perfume permeates the spirit.

Dr. Barrow of Myriad View Artisan Distillery moonlights as a legal moonshiner and an old-school gin maker. His various secret aromatics and botanicals are an elegant liquid complement for my purloined roses. One sip of these cocktails and our guests feel like they fell into a wild rose bush. They can drink their way out with a shot of small-town entrepreneurialism at its best.

Rose Negroni

The mysteriously spicy and subtly bitter flavours of this classic cocktail perfectly complement and balance the aromatic rose.

Serves 2

2 cups (500 mL) ice cubes
2 ounces (60 mL) Rose Gin (page 247) or your favourite premium gin
2 ounces (60 mL) Campari
2 ounces (60 mL) sweet red vermouth
2 cups (500 mL) cracked ice
2 orange twists, for garnish

Half fill a cocktail shaker, or a 4-cup (1 L) mason jar with a lid, with the ice cubes. Add the gin, Campari, and vermouth. Shake vigorously, then strain the nectar into festive cocktail glasses filled with the cracked ice. Garnish with an orange twist.

Rose Gin Fizz

This light and bright summer cocktail allows the pure flavour of rose to shine.

Serves 2

2 cups (500 mL) ice cubes
3 ounces (90 mL) Rose Gin (page 247) or your favourite premium gin
1 ounce (30 mL) Simple Syrup (page 247)
1 ounce (30 mL) freshly squeezed lemon juice
1 ounce (30 mL) egg white (from 1 egg)
6 ounces (170 mL) soda water

Half fill a cocktail shaker, or a 4-cup (1 L) mason jar with a lid, with the ice cubes. Add the gin, simple syrup, lemon juice, and egg white. Shake vigorously until foamy, then strain into coupe glasses. Top with the soda water.

SHUCK YOUR OWN OYSTERS

The fine art of oyster shucking, slurping, chewing, and swallowing is an essential Maritime skill. Setting up and hosting an oyster bar is an awesome party trick. It's respectful of your guests or fellow partygoers. If you can't play the fiddle or piano or stay sober, shuck the oysters. Mastery only comes with experience, so here are a few basic tips to get you started:

- Oysters travel extremely well. Get your hands on some impeccably fresh ones. Visit your trusted fishmonger or arrange to have them shipped directly to your home from a fisher. Expect to pay a premium for this service, but you'll get a premium product.

- Use a sturdy oyster knife. OXO Good Grips makes an excellent knife, but if you prefer the best, Guinness World Record holder Patrick McMurray makes a fine knife too. Patrick custom-moulded a prototype to my hand fifteen years ago, at three in the morning. The rest is history.

- Protect your other hand with a folded tea towel or mesh safety glove. At the inn we prefer black towels, as they hide the mess well at our busy oyster bar. Shucking is messy business.

- Work the blade's tip into the hinge of the shell. The knife works best when you twist it in the hinge like a key in a lock, rather than a lever. Levering breaks the shell.

- The initial pop signals the breaking of a very small hinge muscle that still needs severing. To expose it, release the top shell. Slide your knife along the hidden underside of the top shell, firmly scraping against the shell, cutting through the attached hinge muscle two-thirds of the way to the tip. Repeat on the bottom, ignoring the unattached oyster, focusing on the hinge muscle alone. Again, firmly scrape against the shell with the edge of the blade until you cut through the muscle.

- The briny liquid in the oysters is delicious. In the shucker's code it belongs to the guest, so the pros don't spill a single drop. As you present, encourage your guests to honour the oysters and their fresh juices by slurping loudly.

- As you shuck, steady the oysters and their juices on your towel. To steady a mess of oysters for your guests, shuck and slurp the first one for yourself. Turn both empty shells upside down and place next to each other on a platter or serving surface. Shuck away, using the accumulating empty top shells as a levelling perch for the fully laden bottom shells.

- Shuck, slurp, chew, then swallow. Don't forget to chew. It's the only way to enjoy the pristine flavours and show respect to the oyster and the hard work of its fisher. Those who merely swallow, who believe in the myth of non-chewing, are not true oyster-believers. The rest of us know what all the fuss and ruckus is about.

Tools for Shucking Your Own Oysters: 2 or 3 oyster shucking knives; folded kitchen towels, preferably black to hide the mess; safety glove or heavy-duty work glove for the hand that holds the oyster

BAY FORTUNE OYSTER BAR

BLOODY MARY ICE, SASSY SHUCKING

Oysters are a big deal at the inn. They are an edible introduction to everything we do, representing our profound connection to the sea around us, to our fisherfolk, our bay, and the bounty of our feast. "Slurp all ya like, we're not keeping score!" In our oyster bar, guests hear the legendary call and put us to the test nightly. They also hear a lot of sass as our passionate shuckers rally the crowd while opening more than 500 of our favourite shellfish every night. Each season, year after year, we shuck and slurp more local oysters than ever before, every single one served this way. Icy cold, on the half shell, freshly shucked in front of your eyes, topped with our famous frozen ice. Grown-up slushie on an impeccably fresh oyster served with love and laughter. That's as close to perfection as we get.

It's easy to pull off at home too. Keep a jar of Bloody Mary Ice on standby in the freezer for an oyster party. Or make it the day before, so it's ready to go.

Make the Bloody Mary Ice

In a blender or food processor, combine the tomatoes, vodka, sugar, hot sauce, Worcestershire sauce, lemon zest and juice, and salt. Purée until smooth. Pour into two 2-cup (500 mL) mason jars with lids, cover tightly, and freeze. Every hour or so give the works a good shake until the mixture is frozen solid. You can refreeze leftovers for months.

Shuck the Oysters

When the party begins, gather your fellow shuckers and carefully get to work. Think "key in the lock," not "lever" (see page 76). Your knife works best when you twist it in the hinge of the oyster shell, while levering invariably breaks the shell. The liquor (the briny liquid) in the oyster is delicious and precious. Try not to spill even a single drop. On a festive platter, steady the shucked oysters as you go by alternating upside-down empty top shells with fully laden bottoms. Just before serving, top each oyster with a chilly dollop of the Bloody Mary ice. Slurp, chew, and swallow!

Makes about 6 cups (1.5 L)
Bloody Mary Ice, enough for
12 dozen oysters

BLOODY MARY ICE
1 can (28 ounces/796 mL)
    whole tomatoes
1 cup (250 mL) vodka, aquavit,
    or gin
1 cup (250 mL) sugar
1 tablespoon (15 mL) hot sauce
1 teaspoon (5 mL)
    Worcestershire sauce
Zest and juice of 4 large lemons
¼ teaspoon (1 mL) salt

A few dozen fresh local oysters,
    washed and rinsed

BACK DECK OYSTERS

TRIPLE CITRUS SHOOTERS

On Prince Edward Island, oyster shucking is as common as knot tying, field plowing, and fiddle playing. Off-island, oyster shucking is as impressive a party trick as piano playing, champagne sabring, or the full levitation of an elephant. When a crowd drops by, here's how to simply and spontaneously impress with a mess of oysters and readily available ingredients.

As with all things oyster, it's always best to invite a loved one or two to share the shucking fun. At the peak of the party, rally your friends to make a real splash. No sense toiling away in some back room with no moral support. It's better for the oysters if you shuck in the thick of the action. They'll be fresher. The party will find them wherever they are.

You can present and serve the oysters directly on your kitchen countertop, dining room table, picnic table, or even tailgate. For maximum party points, though, find a festive platter or other rustic surface. Try fresh cedar shingles, large tiles, cutting boards, quarry stone, live-edge lumber, or weathered barnboard.

Gather your fellow shuckers and shuck away (see page 76). As you shuck, invert the accumulating top shells and arrange in a tight, decorative pattern. Carefully nestle the laden bottoms amidst the tops so not a single delicious drop is spilled and wasted. Arrange as closely together as you can.

With your finger over the mouth of the bottle, evenly sprinkle the spirit over the oysters. Zest the orange, lemon, and lime over the oysters. Cut each fruit in half and squeeze and evenly sprinkle the juices through a mesh strainer. Add a dot of hot sauce or a generous dusting of freshly ground pepper. Share. Repeat until you run out of friends or oysters.

Makes enough for 2 dozen oysters (easily doubled or tripled for a party)

2 dozen impeccably fresh oysters from a well-connected fishmonger

GARNISHES
1 or 2 shots of your favourite frozen spirit, such as vodka, gin, or tequila
1 orange
1 lemon
1 lime
Hot sauce or freshly ground pepper

EMBER-ROASTED OYSTERS

LOVE BUTTER

Oysters are always the life of the party. To heat up an extra-special occasion, we like to coax a hot fire into a warm bed of coals ready for super-cool local oysters with red-hot Love Butter. Maybe that's why oyster hour is our guests' favourite time of day. Imagine—a raging hardwood fire patiently subsiding into a thick bed of glowing coals, freshly shucked oysters from the bay out front of the inn nestled in those coals, their fresh juices gently simmering with a shockingly green, scandalously flavoured, yet appropriately named butter. A brief moment of intensely flavoured ecstasy. What could go wrong?

Lovage (see page 40) grows prolifically on our farm. Its intense celery-like flavour and persistent bright green colour make it one of our favourite herbs. Unsurprisingly our love for lovage gave rise to Love Butter. If you can't find lovage, you can substitute green onions (dark green parts only), fresh tarragon, dill, or parsley. Make the Love Butter ahead of time.

Make the Love Butter

Bring a pot of lightly salted water to a rolling boil. Fill a large bowl with the coldest water your taps can muster.

Remove the pot of boiling water from the heat. Working quickly and using a spoon or tongs, plunge the lovage leaves into the just-simmering water, swirling as they immediately brighten and wilt, just 10 seconds or so. Drain through a mesh strainer or colander without pressing. Quickly transfer the leaves to the cold water, swirling and cooling, 30 seconds more. Drain again without pressing. Transfer the wet leaves to a blender. Add the 2 tablespoons (30 mL) cold water. Purée, scraping down the sides once or twice, until bright green and thoroughly smooth. Transfer to a small bowl and refrigerate, uncovered, until cool.

Add the butter to the blender or a food processor. Purée the butter, scraping down the sides once or twice, until smooth. Add the chilled lovage purée and continue processing until smooth. Store in a resealable container in the fridge for up to 1 month.

recipe continues

Makes about 1 cup (250 mL) Love Butter, enough for 4 dozen oysters

Special Equipment Needed:
a large wood fire, its fuel and eventual fiery bed of coals; 2 or 3 oyster shucking knives; 1 or 2 extra-long tongs; heavy-duty work glove for the hand that holds the tongs

LOVE BUTTER
¼ cup (60 mL) fresh lovage leaves
2 tablespoons (30 mL) cold water
1 cup (250 mL) butter, at room temperature

4 dozen impeccably fresh oysters from a well-connected fishmonger

Build a Fire, Shuck, and Roast the Oysters

Build and tend a large fire until it subsides into a thick bed of glowing coals. Meanwhile, shuck the oysters, taking special care not to spill their brine. Steady with the accumulating top shells inverted onto a serving platter. Top each with a teaspoon or so of love butter.

Grasp the edge of a shell with the tip of your tongs and nestle it into the coals. Repeat until the first dozen oysters are cooking. Take vigil as the juices and melted butter mingle, the oysters just barely poaching, 1 to 2 minutes. As soon as the juices simmer gently at the edges of the oysters, they are done. Any longer and they will overcook, shrivel, toughen, and dry out. Carefully remove the oysters from the coals and rest again on the top shells until cool enough to slurp. Enjoy the firm yet still tender texture of a just-poached oyster. Repeat with remaining oysters.

A Safety Note:
What could go wrong? Exploding shells! Forgotten in the fire by a distracted cook. A thicker oyster shell left for too long in a hot bed of coals will eventually dry out and may crack or explode. It's not particularly dangerous, but it is sudden and surprising, and easily avoided by not overcooking the oysters.

HANDMADE TORTILLAS

A lightly toasted old-fashioned handmade tortilla is the foundation of our fire garden taco pit. The creative toppings are the star of the show, but hidden beneath is the real workhorse—the tortilla. Although there are many ways to make tortillas, with varying levels of authenticity, the best way is always handmade from a few simple ingredients. A fresh tortilla is often a revelation for guests accustomed to machine-made blandness. They remind us what we have lost to factory food: the flavourful nuances of heritage ingredients and the delightful inconsistencies of artisanal methods.

In a large bowl, whisk together the flour, cornmeal, chili powder, and salt. Add the lard, crumbling and mixing with your fingers until thoroughly combined. Stir in the water until absorbed. On a lightly floured work surface, turn out the dough and knead until smooth. Wrap the dough with plastic wrap. Rest and relax for at least 20 minutes at room temperature or refrigerate overnight.

Lightly flour a work surface, your hands, a rolling pin, and the dough. For 3-inch (8 cm) tortillas, pinch off a generous tablespoonful of dough and roll between your palms into a small, tight ball. For 8-inch (20 cm) tortillas, divide the dough into 12 pieces. Flatten the ball of dough into a thin, even, round tortilla. Repeat with the remaining dough. Stack the tortillas between layers of parchment paper.

Preheat a large, heavy non-stick skillet or griddle over medium heat. To judge temperature and get a sense of timing, place 1 tortilla on the hot surface and cook until the bottom is lightly blistered and browned, even blackened a bit. It should take about 1 minute. Using a small spatula, flip the tortilla and toast the second side until lightly browned. It should be done in a minute or so. Adjust the temperature as needed. Cook the tortillas in batches without overcrowding the pan. Serve immediately or cool and store in an airtight container at room temperature for up to 2 days.

Makes twelve 8-inch (20 cm) or fifty 3-inch (8 cm) tortillas

2 cups (500 mL) all-purpose flour
1 cup (250 mL) fine cornmeal or whole wheat flour
1 tablespoon (15 mL) chili powder or ground or whole cumin or caraway seeds
½ teaspoon (2 mL) fine sea salt
8 tablespoons (125 mL) pure lard or butter, at room temperature
1 cup (250 mL) water

FIRE GARDEN TACOS

RED LENTIL SMEAR, SPICY SLAW, TODAY'S GRILL

In our fire garden anything can happen on a taco. We love flavourful flexibility and often share a particularly scarce or special ingredient with our guests, who in turn love the chance to try a new flavour. With Handmade Tortillas (page 85) as a base and our simple taco pit formula, you're just a few tasty ideas away from a great taco bar, too. Begin with a freshly toasted tortilla base, anchor the flavours with a smear of hearty, earthy lentils, then nestle in your favourite grilled meat, fish, or vegetable. Top with a complementary spicy, tangy slaw. It's impossible to eat just one, so plan ahead.

Make the Red Lentil Smear

Toss the butter into a medium saucepan over medium-high heat. Swirl gently as it melts, foams, and eventually lightly browns. Reduce the heat to low and stir in the fennel seeds and cumin seeds. Continue stirring as their flavours emerge and brighten and the seeds lightly toast, about 1 minute. Stir in the onion and garlic. Cover tightly and cook, stirring occasionally, until the vegetables are soft and fragrant, 2 or 3 minutes more. Stir in the lentils and water. Bring to a slow, steady simmer, cover tightly, and cook for 10 minutes. Without uncovering, remove from the heat and let sit for another 10 minutes. In a food processor, purée the lentil mixture until smooth. Serve warm or at room temperature. Store in a covered container in the refrigerator for up to 5 days.

Make the Spicy Slaw

Toss together the shredded vegetables. In a large bowl, whisk together the olive oil, cider vinegar, honey, mustard, hot sauce, and salt. Add the shredded vegetables and toss well. Use immediately or cover and refrigerate overnight.

Assemble the Tacos

Lay a dozen or so freshly toasted tortillas on a work surface. Spread a spoonful of lentil smear on each tortilla. Add desired toppings. Top with a tangle of spicy slaw. Finish with a flourish of fresh herbs and/ or edible flowers.

Makes 36 small or 12 large tacos, serves 6 to 12

RED LENTIL SMEAR
2 tablespoons (30 mL) butter or vegetable oil
1 teaspoon (5 mL) fennel seeds
1 teaspoon (5 mL) cumin seeds
1 large yellow onion, minced
2 or 3 garlic cloves, minced
1 cup (250 mL) red lentils (or other lentils or legumes; adjust water accordingly)
2 cups (500 mL) water

SPICY SLAW
1 cup (250 mL) mixed shredded vegetables, such as cabbage, carrots, turnip, or beets
¼ cup (60 mL) extra-virgin olive oil
2 tablespoons (30 mL) cider vinegar, your favourite vinegar, or citrus juice
1 tablespoon (15 mL) pure liquid honey
1 tablespoon (15 mL) yellow or Dijon mustard
1 teaspoon (5 mL) hot sauce
½ teaspoon (2 mL) sea salt

FILLING OPTIONS
1 pound (450 g) or so of your choice of grilled
  meat or fish, sliced into bite-sized pieces (such
  as beef, lamb, pork, goat, chicken, duck,
  turkey, tofu, lobster, salmon, scallops, tuna,
  halibut, eel, or sashimi-grade raw bluefin tuna)
Grilled vegetables (such as eggplant, zucchini,
  cauliflower, broccoli, or green tomatoes)

GARNISHES
Fresh herbs (such as basil, cilantro, mint, dill,
  fennel, shiso, or anise hyssop)
Edible flowers (such as nasturtium, pansy,
  marigold, or chive or squash blossoms)

1 batch Handmade Tortillas (page 85), freshly
  toasted

SEEDY GOUDA CRACKERS

Our signature cracker plays an important part in our nightly production, serving as the base for our signature smoked salmon. The lowly cracker is often the best supporting actor—think of an hors d'oeuvres party without a good cracker—but every now and then there's a plot twist. This is it. A cracker that might just steal the show from whatever sits upon it.

This cracker dough is loaded with spice seeds and locally produced Gouda cheese (see pages 50 and 255). As the cheese bakes it binds the seeds into a crispy cracker that deserves its name in lights.

Make the Starter Dough
In a medium bowl, stir together the flour, water, and yeast. Cover the bowl with plastic wrap and let sit until foamy and frothy, 2 hours or so.

When the starter dough is ready, preheat the oven to 350°F (180°C). Turn on the convection fan if you have one. Line 2 baking sheets with silicone baking mats or lightly oiled parchment paper.

Make the Seedy Spices
In small bowl, combine all the seeds.

Make the Cheese Crackers
Set up a stand mixer fitted with the dough hook. Scrape the frothing starter dough into the mixer bowl. Add the flour, cheese, melted butter, salt, pepper, and seed mixture. Knead on low speed, scraping down the sides once or twice, until a crumbly dough forms, about 5 minutes.

Measure out a tablespoonful or so of dough and roll between your palms into a small, tight ball. On a work surface, use a rolling pin to flatten the dough into a thin, even cracker about 2 inches (5 cm) across. Lift from the work surface with a thin-bladed spatula and arrange on a baking sheet. Repeat with the remaining dough, placing the crackers close together. Bake until evenly golden brown, about 10 minutes. Let the crackers cool on the baking sheets until they are cool enough to handle. Enjoy immediately or store in an airtight container at room temperature for up to 3 days.

Makes about 36 crackers

STARTER DOUGH
¼ cup (60 mL) all-purpose flour
½ cup (125 mL) water
¼ teaspoon (1 mL) active dry yeast

SEEDY SPICES
2 tablespoons (30 mL) anise seeds
2 tablespoons (30 mL) caraway seeds
2 tablespoons (30 mL) coriander seeds
2 tablespoons (30 mL) cumin seeds
2 tablespoons (30 mL) fennel seeds
2 tablespoons (30 mL) poppy seeds
2 tablespoons (30 mL) white sesame seeds
2 tablespoons (30 mL) black sesame seeds

CHEESE CRACKERS
1¾ cups (425 mL) all-purpose flour
6 ounces (170 g) smoked or plain Gouda cheese, grated (about 1½ cups/375 mL)
½ cup (125 mL) butter, melted
1 teaspoon (5 mL) fine sea salt
1 teaspoon (5 mL) freshly ground pepper

HOT-SMOKED SALMON

SPRUCE TIP–CURED, CEDAR-SMOKED

There are many ways to smoke salmon and many choices to be made by the craftsperson. Farmed or wild. Hot or cold. Dry or wet. Wood, coal, or gas. Hardwood or soft. Lump or briquette. Chips or shavings. In our custom indoor and outdoor smokehouses we're honoured to practise the traditions of this ancient craft. We've pushed a few boundaries, made lots of mistakes and a few discoveries, and learned lots of lessons. We forever tinker with our formula, and find this version one of our favourites. Perfect for tinkering on your back deck.

Naturally, we choose to smoke only ethically sourced fish. Our choice, Sustainable Blue, comes from a land-based closed-loop farm in Nova Scotia (see page 255). We encourage you to make sustainable choices too. Check out Ocean Wise, Seafood Watch, or Marine Stewardship Council.

Serve this hot-smoked salmon with Seedy Gouda Crackers (page 88) and Seaweed Aioli (page 249) or in Smoked Salmon Potato Cakes (page 65). You'll find it easily flakes into large chunks, but is not easily sliced like cold-smoked salmon.

Cure the Salmon

Place the salmon skin side down in a baking dish or on a baking sheet. In a food processor, grind together the brown sugar, salt, pepper, and spruce tips until light green and fragrant. Sprinkle the mixture evenly over the entire surface of the fish. Pat with your fingers into a thick, even layer. Cover with plastic wrap laid directly over the fish and let cure in the fridge for 18 to 24 hours. The fish should feel firm to the touch. Gently rinse off the cure under cold running water. Do not dry the fish. Rest at room temperature for a few minutes but smoke as soon as possible.

Smoke the Salmon

Towards the end of the curing time, build and tend an aromatic fire in your smokehouse or patiently craft a thick bed of glowing charcoal or hardwood coals in your backyard grill. Push the fire to one side of your grill. (If using a Big Green Egg, position the plate separator.) Stabilize the heat between 210°F and 250°F (100°C to 120°C). Add a generous handful or three of wood shavings or chips. Position the moist salmon fillet in the smokehouse. Close the lid and smoke,

recipe continues

Makes 1 large fillet

Special Equipment Needed:
backyard smokehouse or enclosed outdoor grill; base fire and coal bed of fragrant hardwood, aromatic fruitwood (such as apple or cherry), or premium lump charcoal; 2 or 3 generous handfuls of cedar shavings, hardwood chips, or fruitwood chips (such as apple or cherry), soaked in water, more as needed; fire pit kit (page 11)

1 skin-on, boneless salmon fillet (2 to 3 pounds/900 g to 1.35 kg)

1 cup (250 mL) tightly packed brown sugar

½ cup (125 mL) kosher salt (I use Morton)

2 tablespoons (30 mL) ground black pepper

4 ounces (115 g) freshly harvested or frozen spruce tips (see page 32) or rosemary, bay leaf, or fennel seeds

infusing the salmon with flavour. After 30 minutes check on the progress, adjusting the fire and adding more wood shavings or chips as needed to keep the fire smouldering. Smoke for at least an hour in total. Check the internal temperature of the salmon: when it reaches 165°F (74°C), it's safely done. If you can keep the smoke smouldering and the heat low so it doesn't dry out the fish, you can smoke the salmon for another hour.

Serve warm. If not serving now, let the salmon cool. Store in an airtight container or wrap in plastic wrap and refrigerate for up to 5 days or freeze for up to 1 month.

CHARCOAL-SEARED BEEF SKEWERS

JALAPEÑO MINT CHIMICHURRI, SEEDY SPRINKLE

These boldly spiced beef skewers are well balanced by spicy hot jalapeño and cool fresh mint. Like any great appetizer, they make a big flavour statement in a little bite.

Charcoal adds as much to this dish as quality beef and distinctive spices. The pure unbridled heat of well-crafted charcoal sears meat like no other heat source. It's such an important ingredient that we make our own charcoal. Hardwood baked without oxygen for an extended time loses water and various volatile compounds that make up smoke. Left behind is pure carbon and the highest heat possible from wood. That searing heat defines the unmistakable flavour of charcoal. If you are using a gas grill, crank it up to the highest heat!

Make the Beef Skewers

Line a baking sheet with parchment paper. In a large bowl, whisk the egg. Add the ground beef and cilantro.

In a small bowl, whisk together the chili powder, cumin, cinnamon, and salt. Add the spices to the beef mixture. Using your fingers, knead and mix together until thoroughly combined. For large skewers, form ¼ cup (60 mL) or so of the mixture around 4 inches (10 cm) of a metal or bamboo skewer. For small skewers, form 2 tablespoons (30 mL) of the mixture around 2 inches (5 cm) of a skewer. Place on the prepared baking sheet. Repeat with the remaining seasoned meat. Cover tightly with plastic wrap and refrigerate for about 1 hour.

Make the Jalapeño Mint Chimichurri

In a food processor, combine the garlic, jalapeño, lemon zest and juice, olive oil, honey, salt, and mint. Process until thoroughly combined but not puréed. Transfer to a small bowl.

Make the Seedy Sprinkle

In a small bowl, stir together all the seeds.

Grill the Beef Skewers

Build a hardwood fire and tend until you have a fierce bed of coals. Alternatively, prepare and preheat your backyard grill, barbecue, or broiler. Lightly oil the beef skewers with spray oil. Grill, turning occasionally, until lightly browned and still juicy, 2 to 3 minutes per side.

recipe continues

Makes 12 large or 24 small skewers

Special Equipment Needed: backyard fire pit, enclosed outdoor grill, or yakitori or hibachi; base fire and coal bed of premium lump charcoal; fire pit kit (page 11); large or small metal or bamboo skewers

BEEF SKEWERS
1 egg
1½ pounds (675 g) medium ground beef
1 cup (250 mL) minced fresh cilantro leaves and tender stems
2 tablespoons (30 mL) chili powder or curry powder
2 tablespoons (30 mL) ground cumin
1 tablespoon (15 mL) cinnamon
1½ teaspoons (7 mL) salt

JALAPEÑO MINT CHIMICHURRI
4 garlic cloves
1 jalapeño pepper, sliced in half lengthwise, white inner pith and seeds removed
Zest and juice of 1 large lemon
½ cup (125 mL) extra-virgin olive oil
1 tablespoon (15 mL) pure liquid honey
½ teaspoon (2 mL) sea salt
2 cups (500 mL) fresh mint leaves and tender stems

To serve, top each skewer with a spoonful of chimichurri. Sprinkle the seed mixture over the skewers.

Serve with:
an array of vegetable side dishes and seasonal salads such as Blue Ribbon Lobster Potato Salad (page 180), June Hodgepodge (page 194), Tomato Marigold Salad (page 201), Sunchoke Fries (page 205), or Summer Salad (page 216)

SEEDY SPRINKLE

1 tablespoon (15 mL) caraway seeds

1 tablespoon (15 mL) coriander seeds

1 tablespoon (15 mL) cumin seeds

1 tablespoon (15 mL) fennel seeds

1 tablespoon (15 mL) poppy seeds

1 tablespoon (15 mL) black sesame seeds

WOOD-ROASTED LAMB

HERB GARDEN BRUSH, MUSTARD BASTE

An entire lamb slowly, patiently roasting over a wood fire for an entire day is not just a tasty feast for the stomach but also a spectacle for the eyes, a respectful send-off for a valued animal, an homage to a farmer, a treat for our cooks, and ultimately the memory of a lifetime for our guests. That's why we take on this challenge. The event and the story, but ultimately the incomparable flavour of respectfully raised meat roasted over a low, smoky fire. The patient cook is rewarded with meltingly tender, deliciously juicy meat.

Start Roasting the Lamb

Using strong wire, firmly attach the lamb to a metal frame or grate strong enough to support its weight. Season generously with salt and pepper.

Build a steady campfire against the back of a smoke shed or against a small fireproof wall for reflected heat. Lean the lamb near but not over the flames, offset from the direct heat but well within enough smoky goodness to slowly cook the meat's many muscles.

Baste with the Mustard Baste

In a medium bowl, whisk together the cider vinegar, mustard, and honey for basting. Pour into 1 or 2 large roasting pans strategically positioned under the lamb to gather its dripping juices. When the meat begins to sizzle and sear, frequently and thoroughly baste with the herb bouquet or a barbecue brush. Continue cooking and basting, rotating the lamb every hour or so to maintain even cooking. Monitor the meat's internal temperature with a digital probe thermometer. The lamb is done when it reaches 145°F (63°C), but truly delicious only after it stays there for a while. Plan at least 4 hours, 6 if you can slow down your fire.

Remove the lamb from the fire and present with as much festive flair as you can to as many family and friends as you can find.

Serve with:
an array of vegetable side dishes and seasonal salads such as Blue Ribbon Lobster Potato Salad (page 180), June Hodgepodge (page 194), Tomato Marigold Salad (page 201), and Summer Salad (page 216)

Serves a crowd (yields 25 to 30 pounds/11.3 to 13.6 kg cooked meat)

Special Equipment Needed:
smoke shed open to the front or a dedicated inflammable wall of dry-stacked concrete blocks, sheet metal, or galvanized steel roofing; large open area free from nearby trees; steady hardwood fire; fire pit kit (page 11)

WOOD-ROASTED LAMB
1 whole lamb, safely butchered, head removed, gutted and split but not halved (about 90 pounds/41 kg)
2 cups (500 mL) kosher salt (I use Morton)
1 cup (250 mL) ground black pepper

MUSTARD BASTE
4 cups (1 L) cider vinegar
2 cups (500 mL) Dijon or yellow mustard
1 cup (250 mL) pure liquid honey
A thick bouquet of fresh herbs with strong stems (sage, rosemary, or tarragon), for basting (optional)

HERBED SAUSAGE

STICKY MUSTARD

Grilled sausages are a universal treat. In the backyards and alleys of the world, you'll always find local ingredients and traditional flavours. Over the fires behind the inn we grill handmade sausages with a global parade of interesting ideas, inspired condiments, and an interactive twist or two. Invite your guests to customize their hors d'oeuvres. Dip freshly grilled sausage skewers in sticky honey mustard, then dredge through your choice of freshly minced herbs. Feel free to use less common herbs such as anise hyssop, lovage, or marigold.

Make the Sticky Mustard

In a small bowl, whisk together the mustard and honey. Transfer to a small bowl big enough for dipping the sausage skewers.

Make the Herbed Sausage

Place each chopped herb in a separate small bowl big enough for coating the sausage skewers.

Meanwhile, build a hardwood fire and tend until you have a fierce bed of coals. Alternatively, preheat a backyard grill, barbecue, or other live-fire heat source.

Grill the sausages, turning once or twice, until lightly browned and still juicy, about 10 minutes. The sausage is safely done when an instant-read thermometer reads 165°F (74°C). Remove and let rest for a few minutes before slicing into bite-sized pieces. Skewer 3 or 4 sausage pieces on each small skewer. Serve the sausage skewers on a platter with the sticky honey mustard and freshly chopped herbs. Dip in the sticky honey mustard, roll in an herb, taste, and repeat.

Serve with:
an array of vegetable side dishes and seasonal salads such as Blue Ribbon Lobster Potato Salad (page 180), June Hodgepodge (page 194), Tomato Marigold Salad (page 201), Sunchoke Fries (page 205), or Summer Salad (page 216)

Serves 8

Special Equipment Needed: backyard fire pit or enclosed outdoor grill; base fire and coal bed of fragrant hardwood, aromatic fruitwood (such as apple or cherry), or premium lump charcoal; fire pit kit (page 11); small skewers

STICKY MUSTARD
¼ cup (60 mL) Dijon, yellow, or grainy mustard
¼ cup (60 mL) pure liquid honey

HERBED SAUSAGE
(CHOOSE YOUR FAVOURITE HERBS; 3 CUPS/750 ML IN TOTAL)
Fresh basil, finely chopped
Fresh mint, finely chopped
Fresh tarragon, finely chopped
Fresh parsley, finely chopped
Fresh dill, finely chopped
Fresh fennel, finely chopped
2 pounds (900 g) fresh sausages

The Feast

RED FIFE BREAD

Every morning we bake naturally fermented bread in our wood-fired oven with the retained heat of yesterday's fires. Over the years, our baker has mastered both the challenges of our oven and baking with exclusively Island-grown heritage grains while nurturing a living dough from wild yeast.

Red Fife was Canada's first grain. As settlers broke sod across the continent, it became the gold standard for milling across the country. Today its genetic descendants are some of the finest wheats in the world, while the original strain has become an artisanal ingredient prized for its rich, nutty flavour. In this patient dough its qualities shine again.

Makes 2 round boules

4 cups (16 ounces/450 g)
    all-purpose flour
2½ cups (10 ounces/300 g) Red
    Fife flour
2 teaspoons (10 mL) sea salt
Heaping ½ teaspoon (3 mL)
    active dry yeast
2 cups (500 mL) water

In a large bowl, whisk together the all-purpose flour, Red Fife flour, salt, and yeast. Add the water. Using the handle of a wooden spoon, stir vigorously, gathering all the flour and forming a ball of dough Tightly cover the bowl with plastic wrap and rest at room temperature for 8 to 12 hours. The dough will strengthen, develop elasticity, and double in size.

Preheat the oven to 425°F (220°C). Turn on the convection fan if you have one. Lightly oil a large baking sheet.

Lightly flour your hands and work surface. Gather the sticky dough from the bowl, deflating it as you turn it out onto the work surface. Cut the dough into 2 equal parts. Knead and roll each half into a firm, tight ball, using only as much additional flour as you need to handle easily. Place the dough balls on the baking sheet. Let sit, uncovered, until the dough doubles in size, about 1 hour.

Bake until deliciously browned and crusty, about 50 minutes. Rest a few minutes before cutting. Cool completely before storing in a plastic bag for up to 3 days.

THE BREAD TREE

MAPLE BROWN BUTTER, MINT FRESH CHEESE, HAPPY PIG PÂTÉ

Our custom iron bread tree whimsically presents our Red Fife Bread (page 103) in its branches with bowls of accompanying spreads nestled in the roots. We slowly brown butter to release its hidden nutty fragrance, then whip it smooth with maple syrup. Milk is gently curdled and crafted into a simple farmer's cheese, then flavoured with one of our favourite mint varieties. Pigs are happily raised for an entire season to be cured and smoked as our signature hams, then braised with cider and puréed with one of the world's finest cheddar cheeses into a exquisite pâté. An artistic masterpiece of form, function, and flavour.

Maple Brown Butter

Smooth whipped butter flavoured with its own richly browned milk-fat solids and sweet fragrant maple syrup.

Makes 3 cups (750 mL)

1 pound (450 g) butter, at room temperature, divided
¼ cup (60 mL) dark pure maple syrup

Place ½ pound (225 g) of the butter in a large saucepan over medium-high heat. Swirl gently as it melts, foams, and eventually lightly browns. Transfer every drop, including the flavourful brown sediment, to a small storage container. Cover tightly and let sit on the counter until cooled to room temperature, a few hours or overnight.

In a stand mixer fitted with the whisk, whip the remaining ½ pound (225 g) butter, scraping down the sides once or twice, until smooth and pale yellow. Scrape in the brown butter and the maple syrup. Whip until smooth. Transfer to a small container for serving. Store, covered, at room temperature for up to 3 days.

Mint Fresh Cheese

On our culinary farm we have discovered that the wrinkly leaves of Kentucky Colonel spearmint do the best job flavouring this cheese while keeping its bright green colour.

Makes 3 cups (750 mL)

FRESH CHEESE
4 cups (1 L) whole milk
1 cup (250 mL) heavy (35%) cream
1 teaspoon (5 mL) sea salt
3 tablespoons (45 mL) white vinegar

MINT PURÉE
¼ cup (60 mL) fresh Kentucky Colonel spearmint (or other varietal) leaves and tender stems

Make the Fresh Cheese

In a large saucepan over high heat, bring the milk, cream, and salt just to a boil, stirring frequently. Remove from the heat and gently stir in the vinegar, continuing to stir until the dairy curdles, no more than a minute. Let sit for 30 minutes. Pour into a fine-mesh strainer lined with several layers of cheesecloth and drain over a large bowl for 1 hour (or cover and let drain in the refrigerator overnight). Reserve the whey for another use. Transfer the cheese to a resealable container and refrigerate until firm.

recipe continues

Make the Mint Purée

Bring a small pot of lightly salted water to a rolling boil. Fill a medium bowl with the coldest water your taps can muster. Set up your high-speed blender and your stand mixer fitted with the whisk.

Working quickly, remove the pot of boiling water from the heat and plunge the mint leaves into the just-simmering water, swirling as they immediately brighten and wilt, just a moment or two. Drain through a mesh strainer or colander without pressing. Quickly transfer the leaves to the cold water, swirling and cooling, a few moments more. Drain again without pressing. Transfer the wet leaves to the blender. Purée, scraping down the sides once or twice, until bright green and thoroughly smooth. Add a splash of cold water if the blender needs some help. Transfer the purée to a small bowl and refrigerate until cool to the touch.

In the stand mixer bowl, combine the cheese and mint purée. Whip until thick and smooth, about 5 minutes. Transfer to a small bowl for serving. Store, covered and refrigerated, for up to 5 days.

Happy Pig Pâté

At the inn, after our guests meet this year's happy pigs, it is a symbolic but important gesture for them to enjoy last year's happy pigs (see page 49) in this pâté.

Makes 2 cups (500 mL)

8 ounces (225 g) boneless artisanal smoked ham
½ cup (125 mL) fresh apple cider
1 tablespoon (15 mL) Dijon mustard
2 teaspoons (10 mL) rubbed sage
4 ounces (115 g) Avonlea Clothbound Cheddar or other artisanal aged white cheddar cheese, grated

Preheat the oven to 300°F (150°C). Cut the ham into large chunks. In a small casserole dish, baking pan, sauté pan, or saucepan, combine the ham with the apple cider and mustard. Cover tightly with a lid or foil and braise until meltingly tender, 2 hours.

Carefully transfer the hot contents to a food processor. Add the sage and process until smooth, scraping down the sides once or twice. Add the cheese and process again until a smooth pâté forms. Transfer to a small bowl for serving. Store, covered and refrigerated, for up to 3 days.

CLASSIC MARITIME CHOWDER

Of the world's many soups, chowder is most closely associated with the shorelines of Maritime Canada and New England. On Prince Edward Island its simplicity has traditionally been a way to enjoy the harvest of the surrounding sea. As an homage to our many fisherfolk, our chowder is crafted with all of our shellfish: mussels, bar clams, lobster, scallops, and crab. (Oysters are too precious for the pot and just end up getting slurped by the cook anyway.) We simmer a classic fish broth, season with salt cod, finish with fresh halibut and fresh cream, and wait patiently for nothing but the starch of the simmering potatoes to thicken the works. Just in case there's not enough flavour, I forage a secret local beach for sea vegetable garnish.

Start the Maritime Chowder
In a small bowl, break the salt cod into a few pieces. Add the milk, cover tightly with plastic wrap, and refrigerate for at least 2 hours or overnight. Drain well, discarding the salty milk. Flake the salt cod into smaller pieces.

Meanwhile, Make the Chowder Broth
In a large pot, combine the fish bones, onion, carrot, celery, bay leaves, thyme, milk, salt, and pepper. Bring to a slow, steady simmer and continue cooking for 30 minutes. Remove from the heat and let rest for 30 minutes. Strain through a mesh strainer set over another large pot or bowl. Discard the vegetables. The broth can be stored, covered and refrigerated, for up to 5 days.

Finish the Maritime Chowder
Toss the bacon into a large soup pot over medium-high heat with a splash of water to help it cook evenly. Cook, stirring frequently, until sizzling hot and lightly crisped but not fully browned, about 5 minutes. Add the onion, carrots, and celery and cook, stirring frequently and without browning, just until the vegetables are sizzling hot and deliciously fragrant, 3 or 4 minutes.

Serves 6 to 8

MARITIME CHOWDER
6 ounces (170 g) salt cod
2 cups (500 mL) whole milk
4 slices bacon, cut crosswise into thin strips
1 large yellow onion, finely diced
1 large carrot, peeled and finely diced
1 stalk celery, finely diced
½ cup (125 mL) dry white wine
1 pound (450 g) fresh mussels, rinsed well and beards removed
1 jar (5 ounces/153 g) clams, drained and juices reserved, chopped
4 cups (1 L) Chowder Broth (recipe ingredients on the next page) or whole milk
2 cups (500 mL) diced peeled Yukon Gold or russet potatoes (2 or 3 potatoes)
1 cup (250 mL) heavy (35%) cream
Meat from 2 cooked lobsters, chopped
6 ounces (170 g) scallops
6 ounces (170 g) crab meat, carefully picked over for any stray bits of shell
6 ounces (170 g) fresh white fish (such as halibut, hake, or haddock)
1 cup (250 mL) minced fresh parsley, chives, lovage, dill, or green onions

recipe continues

Pour in the white wine and add the mussels. Cover tightly with a lid and steam until all the mussels open and the meat within cooks through, 5 minutes or so. Remove the pot from the heat and discard any mussels that did not open. Remove the meat from the shells and reserve. Discard the shells.

To the pot add the reserved clam juice, chowder broth, potatoes, and reserved salt cod. Bring to a simmer and continue to cook until the potatoes are tender, 10 to 15 minutes. Add the cream and return to a simmer.

Stir in the lobster, scallops, crab meat, white fish, and reserved clams and mussel meat. Return to a simmer and simmer until the fish is cooked through, 2 or 3 minutes. Remove from the heat, stir in the parsley, ladle the chowder into bowls, and serve. Leftovers can be covered tightly and refrigerated for up to 3 days before a thorough reheating.

CHOWDER BROTH

2 pounds (900 g) white fish bones or unpeeled frozen shrimp
1 large yellow onion, thinly sliced
1 large carrot, peeled and thinly sliced
1 stalk celery, thinly sliced
2 bay leaves
4 sprigs fresh thyme
4 cups (1 L) whole milk or water
1 teaspoon (5 mL) sea salt
Freshly ground pepper

Serve with:
Red Fife Bread (page 103)

Maple Brown Butter (page 105)

WOOD-ROASTED CHICKEN AND FARM VEGETABLE SOUP

Every chicken is a myriad of meals waiting to happen. One of my favourites is a simple old-fashioned farmhouse soup. One bird patiently transformed into a meal for many. On Prince Edward Island, every cook knew how to turn a yard bird into enough soup for a tableful of hungry mouths. The best cooks also knew how to build flavour every step of the way. Spatchcocking the bird doubles its surface area and doubles its golden-brown flavour. In our wood oven, humble ingredients are transformed by high heat and aromatic smoke before simmering into a deeply flavoured broth brimming with farm-fresh vegetables and bright green herbs. The method is detailed but the results are deeply, richly worth it.

Fire up your wood oven, banking a crackling hardwood fire to one side. Alternatively, preheat the oven to 425°F (220°C). Turn on the convection fan if you have one. Preheat a large cast-iron skillet or roasting pan.

Spatchcock the Chicken
Lay the chicken breast side down. With a pair of sharp kitchen shears cut along each side of the backbone, removing it and the attached neck. Turn the bird over and firmly press down on the breastbone and legs, flattening the bird as best you can. Season generously with salt and pepper.

Make the Wood-Roasted Broth
Carefully place the chicken, skin side up, in the preheated pan. Nestle the onions, carrots, parsnips, celery, and garlic cloves around the bird, filling the pan. Return to the oven and begin roasting. After 30 minutes, firmly swirl and shake the pan, evenly coating the vegetables with flavourful juices. Continue roasting until the chicken is crispy, golden brown, and fragrant, about another hour.

Remove the chicken from the oven. Carefully pour off and reserve as much of the rendered fat as possible. Using 2 metal tongs, pick, tug, and shred off as much of the roast meat and skin as you can. Cover the meat tightly and refrigerate to use in the soup. Remove and

recipe continues

Serves 6 to 8

Special Equipment Needed:
preheated wood oven, base fire and coal bed of fragrant hardwood or aromatic fruitwood (such as apple or cherry); fire pit kit (page 11)

WOOD-ROASTED CHICKEN BROTH
1 large roasting chicken (about 5 pounds/2.25 kg)
1 tablespoon (15 mL) sea salt
Freshly ground pepper
4 large white or yellow onions, chopped
2 large carrots, peeled and thinly sliced
2 parsnips, peeled and thinly sliced
2 stalks celery, thinly sliced
Cloves from 1 head of garlic, crushed
12 cups (3 L) water, divided
12 sprigs fresh thyme
4 sprigs fresh rosemary
2 bay leaves

reserve the roasted vegetables. Flip the carcass over, exposing the inside. Pour 1 cup (250 mL) or so of the water into the pan, shaking the works to evenly distribute the juices. Return the pan to the oven and continue cooking until the meaty remnants are browned, about 30 minutes.

Remove the pan from the oven. Pour 4 cups (1 L) of the water into the pan. Carefully transfer the chicken carcass and the reserved roasted vegetables to a large soup or stock pot. While the water is still in the pan, stir until every single flavourful browned bit has dissolved. Scrape every last drop into the pot. Pour in the remaining 7 cups (1.75 L) water. Toss in the thyme, rosemary, and bay leaves. Cover tightly and bring to a slow, steady simmer. Stir occasionally and continue simmering until rich and fragrant, an hour or so. Remove from the heat and let rest for an hour. Strain the broth through a fine-mesh strainer and reserve. Discard the solids.

Make the Farm Vegetable Soup

Pour the reserved chicken fat into the soup pot over medium-high heat. Add the onions, carrots, parsnips, celery, and salt. Cook over medium-high heat, stirring frequently as the vegetables' flavours brighten and their textures soften, about 5 minutes. Add the potatoes and the reserved chicken broth and meat. Cover tightly and reduce the heat to a simmer. Continue simmering until the potatoes are tender, 15 minutes or so. Taste and adjust the salt and pepper if you like. Stir in the parsley, chives, and tarragon. Ladle into bowls and serve.

FARM VEGETABLE SOUP

2 white or yellow onions, finely diced

2 large carrots, peeled and finely diced

2 parsnips, peeled and finely diced

2 stalks celery, finely diced

1 teaspoon (5 mL) sea salt

2 large potatoes, peeled and diced

½ cup (125 mL) flat-leaf or curly parsley leaves and tender stems, finely chopped

½ cup (125 mL) fresh chives or green onion tops, very thinly sliced

2 tablespoons (30 mL) minced fresh tarragon

VEGETABLE CAKES

RHUBARB CHUTNEY, LENTIL SPROUT RAITA

The FireWorks Feast at the inn is farm-focused, plant-based, and vegetable-forward, so we easily accommodate our many vegetarian guests with what they often describe as the meal of the lifetime. This centre-of-the-plate signature is stuffed with nutritional density, gluten-free status, and impeccable vegetarian credentials (leave out the raita if you avoid dairy). We include both brown rice and lentils for their earthy flavour and as a complete vegetable protein, and mushrooms and various savoury seasonings add underlying umami. But chia seeds are the secret ingredient. They bind the moisture of the mix while adding strong body to the texture. We're proud to offer this cake nightly with an artful array of ever-evolving condiments, farm flavours, and inspired ideas.

Make the Vegetarian Base

In a large skillet, heat the vegetable oil over medium-high heat. Toss in the onion and garlic and sauté until they just begin to lightly colour, 2 or 3 minutes. Add the mushrooms, cover tightly, and continue cooking, stirring occasionally, until the mushrooms release their earthy moisture, about 10 minutes. Stir in the brown rice, lentils, water, rosemary, and bay leaf. Bring to a slow, steady simmer. Cover and continue cooking, stirring occasionally, until the rice and lentils are tender, about 30 minutes. Remove from the heat and rest for 10 minutes without uncovering.

Make the Cake Blend

Spoon the vegetarian base into a food processor. Add the chia seeds, peanut butter, miso paste, and soy sauce. Pulse until smooth, scraping down the sides once or twice. Transfer to a large bowl and stir in the sweet potato by hand. Cover with plastic wrap and refrigerate and rest, giving the chia seeds time to work their magic, absorbing, swelling, and strengthening the protein-rich savoury blend, at least 1 hour or overnight.

Makes 8 cakes

VEGETARIAN BASE
2 tablespoons (30 mL) vegetable oil or olive oil
1 yellow onion, finely chopped
Cloves from 1 head of garlic, finely minced
1 pound (450 g) mushrooms (a single type or a blend of varieties such as cremini, portobello, oyster, chanterelle, and king), sliced
1 cup (250 mL) brown rice
1 cup (250 mL) green lentils
2½ cups (625 mL) water
2 tablespoons (30 mL) finely minced fresh rosemary
1 bay leaf

CAKE BLEND
1 cup (250 mL) chia seeds
½ cup (125 mL) smoked peanut butter or your favourite nut butter
2 tablespoons (30 mL) miso paste
2 tablespoons (30 mL) soy sauce
1 sweet potato, peeled and grated

recipe continues

Meanwhile, Make the Lentil Sprout Raita

Combine the coriander seeds, cumin seeds, and fennel seeds in a medium skillet. Swirl and toss over medium-high heat until the seeds are lightly toasted and fragrant, a minute or so. Transfer to a medium bowl. Stir in the yogurt, lemon zest and juice, and honey. Just before serving, add the lentil sprouts and mint and lightly toss to combine. Enjoy fresh.

Cook the Cakes

Preheat the oven to 400°F (200°C). Turn on the convection fan if you have one. Line a baking sheet with parchment paper and lightly oil it.

Using your hands, divide the cake blend into 8 equal portions and form into evenly shaped cakes about 1 inch (2.5 cm) thick. Place the cakes on the prepared baking sheet and bake until firm, 20 minutes or so. Alternatively, pan-fry in a lightly oiled non-stick pan.

Serve as a full vegetarian meal with the lentil sprout raita and rhubarb chutney, a simple tangle of tangy greens, or your favourite vegetarian condiments and sides.

LENTIL SPROUT RAITA

1 teaspoon (5 mL) coriander seeds

1 teaspoon (5 mL) cumin seeds

1 teaspoon (5 mL) fennel seeds

½ cup (125 mL) natural plain full-fat yogurt or a dairy-free alternative, if needed

Zest and juice of 1 lemon

1 tablespoon (15 mL) pure liquid honey

2 cups (500 mL) freshly harvested lentil sprouts (page 117) or store-bought

1 cup (250 mL) fresh mint leaves, thinly sliced (1 bunch)

Rhubarb Chutney (page 250), for serving

FARM HARVEST BOWL AND EARTH PLATE

LIQUID SUNSHINE DRESSING, SEEDY SOIL, ASH-BAKED BEET PURÉE, WOOD-ROASTED CARROT PURÉE, SMOKED TURNIP PURÉE, LENTIL SPROUTS

We're intensely proud of our farm and love sharing its bounty through our salad course ceremony. Each guest's Earth Plate grounds the presentation with three different root vegetable purées, crunchy seedy soil, and living sprouts. In the shared Farm Harvest Bowl, we toss together as many bright, interesting flavours as we can: shoots, stems, stalks, leaves, herbs, buds, flowers, and fruits from our farm. Our famous house dressing features local cider vinegar and fragrant liquid sunshine, Island-grown extra-virgin canola oil. Every bite comes from above and below the soil and is as unique as our farm.

Lentil Sprouts

Our Earth Plate would not be complete without living sprouts. Ounce for ounce, lentil sprouts are one of the most nutrient-dense foods we harvest. You can buy sprouted lentils, but it's well worth the effort to go the extra mile and sprout your own. You'll be amazed at how simple it is to do and you'll love their sweet fresh flavour.

¼ cup (60 mL) green or brown lentils

Start sprouting the lentils 5 days in advance. Cut a piece of mesh screen about 4 inches (10 cm) square. Pour the lentils into a 1-quart (1 L) mason jar. Cover the jar's mouth with the screen and tighten on the screw ring (don't use the flat lid). This will make it super easy to rinse and drain your sprouts. Fill the jar with water, drain it through the mesh, and fill it again. Soak the lentils for 4 hours or so, then drain well.

Start a twice-daily routine for your lentil babies. Each morning and evening, gently fill the jar with fresh water, rinse the lentils, then drain well through the screen. Try not to let the lentils sit in the water. Rest the jar on its side on a kitchen windowsill. The lentils are starting to grow already, even though you can't see it.

Shortly after the first day, they'll begin to sprout. In just 2 or 3 days, the sprouts will be about ½ inch (1 cm) long, with small green leaves

recipe continues

Serves 4 to 6

Special Equipment Needed:
backyard smokehouse or enclosed outdoor grill; base fire and coal bed of fragrant hardwood, aromatic fruitwood (such as apple or cherry), or premium lump charcoal; 2 or 3 generous handfuls of cedar shavings, hardwood chips, or fruitwood chips (such as apple or cherry), soaked in water, more as needed; fire pit kit (page 11)

PREP AND PLAN
- Start the lentil sprouts 5 days before you need them.
- Make the Seedy Soil up to a week in advance.
- Make the root vegetable purées 1 or 2 days in advance.
- If you can, gather your harvest bowl greens and garnishes the same day you serve them.
- Make the Liquid Sunshine Dressing just before serving.

forming on the ends. You can eat them now or save them for later. To save, swap the screen for the jar's lid and refrigerate for up to a week.

Seedy Soil

This Earth Plate garnish brings fragrant crunch to our salad and is often one of our guests' favourites tastes of the evening. The caramelized spice seeds add delicious bursts of texture to the edible "soil" made from our oatmeal bread.

OATMEAL BREAD
¾ cup (175 mL) large-flake oats, gluten-free if required
1 cup (250 mL) buckwheat flour
1 teaspoon (5 mL) baking powder
½ teaspoon (2 mL) sea salt
½ cup (125 mL) water
1 tablespoon (15 mL) extra-virgin canola oil or olive oil

SEEDY SOIL
1 tablespoon (15 mL) caraway seeds
1 tablespoon (15 mL) coriander seeds
1 tablespoon (15 mL) cumin seeds
1 tablespoon (15 mL) dill seeds
1 tablespoon (15 mL) fennel seeds
1 tablespoon (15 mL) pink peppercorns
½ teaspoon (2 mL) baking soda
½ cup (125 mL) water
½ cup (125 mL) sugar
2 cups (500 mL) Oatmeal Bread crumbs

Make the Oatmeal Bread
Preheat the oven to 350°F (180°C). Line a baking sheet with a silicone baking mat or parchment paper.

In a stand mixer fitted with the dough hook, combine the oats, buckwheat flour, baking powder, and salt. Add the water and canola oil. Knead on low speed until a strong dough develops, 2 or 3 minutes. Transfer the dough to the baking sheet and shape with your hands into an even disc about 2 inches (5 cm) thick. Bake until fragrant and browned, about 1 hour. Transfer the loaf to a rack and let rest until cool enough to handle. Keep the oven at 350°F (180°C).

Using your hands, crumble the bread into the bowl of a food processor. Pulse briefly, just until ground into coarse, even crumbs. Spread out the crumbs on the baking sheet and bake, stirring once or twice, until crisp and golden brown, 45 minutes. Let cool. Reserve 2 cups (500 mL) of the breadcrumbs. Store in an airtight container at room temperature for up to a week.

Make the Seedy Soil
Line a baking sheet with parchment paper, foil, or a silicone baking mat. Lightly spray with cooking oil.

In a small bowl, stir together the caraway seeds, coriander seeds, cumin seeds, dill seeds, fennel seeds, pink peppercorns, and baking soda.

Pour the water into a medium saucepan. Carefully pour the sugar into the centre of the pan, being careful to avoid the edges. Without stirring, bring the syrup to a steady simmer over medium-high heat and continue cooking until the water evaporates and the sugar begins caramelizing. Swirl gently until golden brown and fragrant, about 5 minutes.

Remove the syrup from the heat and quickly stir in the seed mixture. Toast until impressively foamed and deliciously fragrant, just a minute. Pour the mixture onto the prepared baking sheet. Cool to room temperature, about 1 hour. Break the candied seeds into pieces and transfer to a food processor. Pulse briefly, just until evenly ground into a coarse powder. Stir together with the reserved 2 cups (500 mL) oatmeal bread crumbs. Reserve the mixture in an airtight storage container at room temperature for up to a week.

Ash-Baked Beet Purée

The Earth Plate represents our farm's soil, and so we garnish it with seeds, sprouts, and flavourful root vegetable purées. Each purée adds dramatic colour and a FireWorks technique, such as beets baked in the dying embers of a fire.

Makes 2 cups (500 mL)

1 pound (450 g) red beets, unpeeled, trimmed and washed
2 tablespoons (30 mL) vegetable oil or olive oil
1 tablespoon (15 mL) sherry vinegar or your favourite vinegar
1 teaspoon (5 mL) sea salt
¾ cup (175 mL) fresh beet juice, divided

Half fill a cast-iron Dutch oven with the live ashes and glowing coals of a finished fire. Bury the beets in the ashes and coals, cover tightly, and rest in a warm place. The residual heat will cook the beets and, with luck and practice, lightly char the flesh just below their skin. Alternatively, bake in a 350°F (180°C) oven. The beets are done when a knife easily pierces them, about 1 hour. Remove the beets with tongs. When cool enough to handle, rinse quickly under cool running water, then carefully wipe away the skin with your fingers.

Transfer the beets to a high-speed blender. Measure in the vegetable oil, sherry vinegar, salt, and ½ cup (125 mL) of the beet juice. Process into a smooth, thick purée, adding up to ¼ cup (60 mL) remaining beet juice if too thick. Transfer to a small storage container and refrigerate.

Wood-Roasted Carrot Purée

The Earth Plate grounds our salad with various seeds and roots. Wood-roasting carrots deliciously caramelizes the natural sugars that all roots contain.

Makes 2 cups (500 mL)

1 pound (450 g) carrots, peeled and cut into large chunks
4 tablespoons (60 mL) vegetable oil or olive oil, divided
2 cups (500 mL) fresh carrot juice, divided
1 tablespoon (30 mL) cider vinegar or sherry vinegar
1 teaspoon (15 mL) sea salt

In a medium cast-iron skillet, toss together the carrots and 1 tablespoon (15 mL) of the vegetable oil. Roast in a live-fire wood oven until browned, about 30 minutes. Alternatively, roast in a 400°F (200°C) oven with the convection fan turned on.

Transfer the carrots to a small saucepan and add 1 cup (250 mL) of the carrot juice. Stirring, bring to a simmer over medium heat. Cover tightly with a lid, remove from the heat, and rest until the carrots are softened, 30 minutes.

Transfer the carrots and their liquid to a high-speed blender. Add the remaining 3 tablespoons (45 mL) vegetable oil, cider vinegar, salt, and the remaining 1 cup (250 mL) carrot juice. Process into a smooth, thick purée. Transfer to a small storage container and refrigerate.

recipe continues

Smoked Parsnip Purée

Parsnips, like most milder white vegetables, are a great choice for highlighting smoky flavours.

Makes 2 cups (500 mL)

1 pound (450 g) parsnips, peeled (reserve peels)
¼ cup (60 mL) vegetable oil or olive oil
1 teaspoon (5 mL) sea salt

Set a steamer basket in a pot filled with about an inch of simmering water. Add the parsnips, cover tightly, and steam until tender in the thickest parts, 15 minutes or so. Alternatively, boil until tender.

Meanwhile, build and tend an aromatic fire in your smokehouse or patiently craft a thick bed of glowing charcoal or hardwood coals in your backyard grill. Push the fire to one side of your grill. (If using a Big Green Egg, position the plate separator.) Stabilize the heat between 210°F and 250°F (100°C to 120°C). Add a generous handful or three of wood shavings or chips. Position the moist parsnips in the smokehouse. Close the lid and smoke, infusing them with flavour. After 30 minutes check on the progress, adjusting the fire and adding more wood shavings or chips as needed to keep the fire smouldering. Smoke until fragrant but not dried out, about 1 hour.

Meanwhile, simmer the reserved parsnip peels in 2 cups (500 mL) of water for a few minutes. Strain, reserving the infusion.

Transfer the smoked parsnips to a high-speed blender and add the vegetable oil, salt, and 1 cup (250 mL) of the parsnip peel infusion. Process into a smooth, thick purée, adding more of the infusion if too thick. Transfer to a small storage container and refrigerate.

Farm Harvest Bowl

The secret to our salad is impeccable freshness and amazing variety. We often have more than fifty different ingredients from our farm in the mix. For best results, source your greens from a few different sources: get to know your farmers' market, grow your own garden, or raid a friend's.

Lettuces
Several handfuls of various lettuces, baby greens, tender leaves, and vegetables

Herbs (lots of freshly picked aromatic herbs, optional choices)

Fresh basil leaves	Anise hyssop leaves
Fresh mint leaves	Lemon balm leaves
Fresh dill leaves	Marigold leaves
Fresh parsley leaves	Nasturtium leaves
Fresh cilantro leaves	Shiso
Fresh fennel fronds	

Microgreens
Vegetable shoots or sprouts such as broccoli, radish, mustard, chard, kale, sunflower, pea, cress

Foraged flavours (optional choices)

Watercress	Lily shoots
Pineapple weed	Cattail shoots
Yarrow	Fireweed shoots
Dandelion greens	

Edible flowers (optional choices)

Nasturtium	Dill
Marigold	Fennel
Chive	Arugula
Borage	Violet

Liquid Sunshine Dressing

This simple dressing allows the nutty fragrance of our liquid sunshine, Island-grown canola oil, to shine. Its high vinegar ratio complements the variety, freshness, and flavours of our farmed greens.

Makes about 1 cup (250 mL)

½ cup (125 mL) extra-virgin canola oil
½ cup (125 mL) apple cider vinegar or pear vinegar
2 tablespoons (30 mL) of your favourite mustard
¼ cup (60 mL) pure liquid honey or pure maple syrup
1 teaspoon (5 mL) Spruce Salt (page 248)
Freshly ground pepper

Just before serving, measure the ingredients into a standard mason jar and shake vigorously until thoroughly mixed and smoothly combined.

PLATE AND PRESENTATION

- One at a time, spoon and swoosh the Ash-Baked Beet Purée, Wood-Roasted Carrot Purée, and Smoked Parsnip Purée onto the plates. At the inn, for full effect we garnish each purée with a pickled version of the same root and a tangle of that root's sprouted seeds.
- Add a heaping spoonful of Seedy Soil.
- Sprinkle with homegrown lentil sprouts or microgreens.
- Gently and thoroughly toss the greens with the Liquid Sunshine Dressing. Share the Farm Harvest Bowl communally so guests can top their own Earth Plate with greens.

RED LENTIL FRITTERS

TOMATO ANCHO CHUTNEY

As a chef, I've had the good fortune to travel the globe looking for flavours and techniques. I stumbled onto this legume fritter in the world's tallest building, Dubai's Burj Khalifa. Fortunately, I kept my footing while a chef buddy shared his simple technique. Back home we make these proudly with Canadian lentils—the best in the world—and always have a batch on hand, ready to serve as a bread substitute for our gluten-free guests. One bite and they quickly realize they've received something special.

This moist batter holds together because of the ability of split red lentils to quickly hydrate (splitting removes their tough hull) and just as quickly bind together as they cook. The batter fries into a perfect fritter, with a crispy exterior and a moist, chewy interior. The fritters pair nicely with an array of farm-focused condiments.

In a medium bowl, stir together the lentils, water, and salt. Cover tightly and soak for at least 1 hour, even overnight. Drain the lentils and transfer to a high-speed blender or food processor. Add the onion and garlic and purée until very smooth. Leave the purée in the blender.

Measure the coriander seeds, cumin seeds, and fennel seeds into a dry medium skillet over medium-high heat. Swirl and toss, heating until lightly toasted and fragrant, a minute or so. Add to the lentil mixture. Pulse briefly to stir the mixture together. Transfer to a medium bowl.

To fry the fritters, pour 2 to 3 inches (5 to 8 cm) of vegetable oil into a deep-fryer or large pot. Carefully heat the oil over medium heat until it reaches 365°F (185°C) on a deep-fat thermometer.

Using 2 spoons, the first to scoop, the second to release the batter, gently drop large dollops of the batter into the hot oil. Work in batches so you don't crowd the pan. Stir gently until the fritters are cooked through and lightly browned, 4 or 5 minutes. Drain briefly on paper towels. Serve lightly salted as an appetizer with tomato ancho chutney or your favourite farm-forward condiment.

Makes 24 large fritters

1 cup (250 mL) red lentils
1 cup (250 mL) water
½ teaspoon (2 mL) sea salt
1 yellow onion, chopped
4 garlic cloves
1 teaspoon (5 mL) coriander seeds
1 teaspoon (5 mL) cumin seeds
1 teaspoon (5 mL) fennel seeds
Vegetable oil, for frying

Tomato Ancho Chutney (page 250), for serving

Today's Catch

BEACH LOBSTER

SEAWATER-POACHED, LEMON BROWN BUTTER

There are many ways to enjoy lobster on Prince Edward Island—from the sea-splashed back deck of the boat that caught it to the crisp white tables of fine-dining restaurants. At the FireWorks Feast we often poach it restaurant style, just enough to firm and release the near-raw meat from the shell before adding various creative flavours and flourishes as we finish cooking it. It's very labour intensive, but we don't mind. So when our cooks take a day off from the crowds and head for a local beach, this is their favourite way to enjoy lobster. Simply poached in fresh seawater, and served with lots of butter. And not just melted butter, but brown butter! They're cooks, they know a few secrets. You will too after you share a lobster with someone you love on an uncrowded beach (easy to find on Prince Edward Island) on a cerulean-blue summer day. Remember to pack beverages for everyone!

Build a Beach Fire

Position the cinder blocks so they'll firmly support the grille and a full pot of water on top but allow lots of room underneath for a fire. Build a campfire ring if you can with stones. Build a large fire between the cinder blocks. Patiently tend into a fierce bed of glowing coals. Position the grille over the cinder blocks. With the shovel, bank the coals directly under the grate to increase the heat. Fill one pot three-quarters or so with freshly foraged seawater. Fill the second pot or the pail with more cold seawater. Tend the fire until the water is boiling. Enjoy a beverage while you wait.

Make the Lemon Brown Butter

Meanwhile, position a small saucepan over the fire and toss in the butter. Swirl gently as it melts, foams, and eventually lightly browns. Remove from the fire and swirl in the lemon zest and juice and the hot sauce. Reserve.

recipe continues

Serves a crowd

Special Equipment Needed (pack for the beach):
2 large pots, 3 gallons (12 L) or more (or 1 pot and 1 pail); small saucepan; picnic cooler to haul your kitchen kit; hard- or softwood and kindling from your home woodpile or random driftwood; 2 standard cinder blocks, 8 × 8 × 16 inches (20 × 20 × 40 cm); large metal barbecue grille; metal shovel or garden spade; fire pit kit (page 11)

Fresh local seawater, or fill the pot with hot tap water, adding 1.3 ounces (35 g) of sea salt per quart (litre)
2 or 3 fresh lobsters per person

LEMON BROWN BUTTER
1 pound (450 g) butter
Zest and juice of 2 lemons
A splash of hot sauce

Boil the Lobster

Pick up a lobster and grasp the claws firmly with your two hands. Cross them and with one hand hold them tightly together at the knuckles, under the claws. With your other hand, tug and slide the rubber bands off the claws. Immediately plunge the lobster into the boiling water. Repeat with a few more lobsters, but don't overwhelm the boiling water with more than a dozen or so at a time.

Quickly return the water to a boil and cook the lobsters for 10 minutes. Using tongs, remove the red lobsters from the water and immediately plunge them into cold seawater for 1 to 2 minutes. Remove and drain. Propose a toast to your good fortune and enjoy. Serve with the lemon brown butter for dipping.

Serve with:
Potato Bacon Cheddar Tart (page 183)

Summer Salad (page 216)

BACON BEER MUSSELS

FIRE TOAST

This campfire favourite is a spectacular way to show how tasty mussels are and how easy they are to cook. On Prince Edward Island, we are blessed with a thriving cultured-mussel fishery. Their buoys dot our bays as a visible reminder of the pristine coastal waters they are raised in. Since mussels travel so well, about 99 percent head off-island, some no doubt to a store near you. Our guests enjoy the mussels that stay behind in big batches meant to be shared. We soak up the savoury broth with delicious rustic bread transformed by fire-toasting.

At the inn we steam mussels in cast-iron cauldrons over live fire, but the results are equally good over any heat source.

Build a Fire and Cook the Mussels

Build and tend an aromatic fire in your backyard, or fire up your barbecue or grill. Alternatively, use your indoor stove.

Toss the bacon into a large soup pot (over medium-high heat if using your stove) with a splash of water to help it cook evenly. Stir frequently until sizzling hot, brown, and crispy, 5 minutes or so. Add the onion and garlic. Sauté until sizzling and fragrant, a minute or two. Pour in the beer and add the thyme and hot sauce. Add the mussels. Cover tightly. Steam, cooking the mussels until they open their shells and release their rich, fragrant broth, about 10 minutes. Discard any mussels that did not open.

Meanwhile, Make the Fire Toast

Lightly brush both sides of the bread slices with the olive oil and grill, turning once or twice, until lightly charred, 2 or 3 minutes per side. Firmly rub and perfume the coarse surface with a whole garlic clove.

Divide the mussels among bowls. Pour in the tasty broth. Sprinkle chives on top. Serve with lots of fire toast for soaking up the broth.

Serves 4 to 6 as a meal, 12 or more as an appetizer

Special Equipment Needed:
backyard fire pit or enclosed outdoor grill or barbecue; base fire and coal bed of fragrant hardwood (such as maple, birch, oak, or hickory) or aromatic fruitwood (such as apple or cherry); fire pit kit (page 11)

BACON BEER MUSSELS
4 to 6 thick slices of bacon, sliced crosswise into thin strips
1 large yellow onion, finely diced
Cloves from 1 head of garlic, thinly sliced
1 bottle (12 ounces/355 mL) of your favourite beer or a large glass of red or white wine
A few sprigs fresh thyme, rosemary, tarragon, or oregano
1 teaspoon (5 mL) hot sauce
5 pounds (2.25 kg) fresh mussels, rinsed well and beards removed
A handful of fresh chives or a few green onions, thinly sliced

FIRE TOAST
1 loaf of your favourite rustic bread, cut into thick slices
¼ cup (60 mL) extra-virgin olive oil
1 or 2 large garlic cloves, peeled

OVEN-BAKED SALT-CRUSTED HALIBUT

PARSLEY PISTOU, OLD-SCHOOL LEMON

On Prince Edward Island, an old lobster-processing plant has been reborn as a sustainable fish farm with a niche product—they raise baby halibut.

Salt-baking is an ancient method to cook an entire fish. Baking in an impermeable casing deliciously steams and aromatically perfumes the delicate flesh while sealing in moisture. You'll need a hammer to crack the salt crust for a show-stopping reveal. Of course, you'll also need a crowd to witness such gourmet mayhem, so wait for a special occasion, rally the troops, and time your reveal for maximum effect. Old-school lemon wedges and fresh parsley pistou add just the right bright aromatic finish.

Make the Salt-Crusted Halibut

Preheat the oven to 400°F (200°C). Turn on the convection fan if you have one. Line a baking sheet with parchment paper or foil.

In a large bowl, lightly whisk the egg whites. Add the kosher salt and stir until it resembles moist sand. Spread a little less than half of the salt mixture in the middle of the baking sheet. Lay a few of the herb sprigs along the middle. Lay the fish on top. Stuff a few more sprigs inside the fish and cover with the remaining sprigs. Top with the remaining salt mixture, completely and evenly covering the fish. Bake the fish until an instant-read thermometer inserted in the thickest part reads 145°F (63°C), 30 to 40 minutes.

Meanwhile, Make the Parsley Pistou

Fill a medium bowl with ice water. Bring a large pot of salted water to a boil. Reserve a few sprigs of parsley for the lemon garnish. Briefly plunge the rest of the parsley into the boiling water, swirling once or twice as it immediately brightens. Using a skimmer or slotted spoon, immediately remove the parsley and plunge it into the ice water, swirling and cooling rapidly. Drain and transfer to a high-speed blender with the garlic, olive oil, and hot sauce. Process until smooth. If your blender struggles, add a splash of water. Scrape the mixture into a small bowl and reserve.

Finely mince the reserved parsley. Sprinkle some paprika on a small plate. Dredge one face of each lemon wedge into the paprika, then the other face into the parsley.

recipe continues

Serves 6 to 8

SALT-CRUSTED HALIBUT
16 egg whites
16 cups (4 L) coarse kosher salt
A handful of fresh herb sprigs (thyme, tarragon, dill, lovage, rosemary, or oregano)
1 whole farm-raised halibut, trout, Arctic char, or other whole fish (8 to 10 pounds/ 3.5 to 4.5 kg), gutted and cleaned, head on
Sweet or smoked paprika or Old Bay seasoning
2 lemons, each cut into 8 wedges
Flaky salt, for finishing
Lots of freshly ground pepper

PARSLEY PISTOU
1 large bunch of flat-leaf or curly parsley
4 garlic cloves
¼ cup (60 mL) extra-virgin olive oil
A few dashes of hot sauce

Serve with:
Hasselback Potatoes (page 175)

Fire-Kissed Bok Choy (page 206)

When the fish is done, remove from the oven and rest for 10 minutes or so. Firmly crack the top crust and carefully remove and discard. Remove and discard the skin from the top of the fish. With a spatula, carefully transfer the top fillets to a serving platter. Either tug out the backbone or flip the fish over and repeat. Have a taste. Surprisingly, you'll find the moist fish under-seasoned, so sprinkle generously with flaky sea salt and freshly ground pepper. Serve with the parsley pistou and lemon wedges.

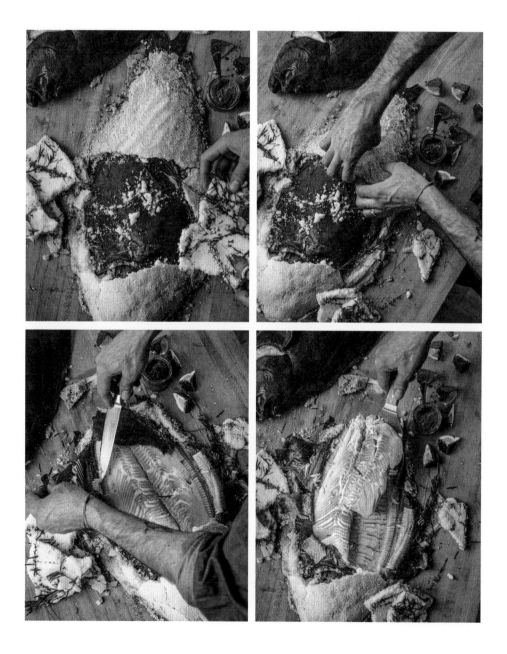

IRON-SEARED HALIBUT AND WILD CHANTERELLES

CHANTERELLE, LENTIL, AND SINGLE MALT SCOTCH STEW, BROWN BUTTER SHERRY CHANTERELLE PURÉE, NUTMEG-PICKLED CHANTERELLES, SEA VEGETABLE SALAD

On Prince Edward Island, wild halibut and chanterelle mushroom seasons overlap every summer for a month or so of flavourful harmony. This sustainably harvested wild fish's characteristic mild flavour comes from its naturally low oil content, which makes its firm white flesh prone to quickly drying out and sticking to a pan. That's why it's often gently poached, but if you can handle the heat, searing adds browned flavour and crispy texture. Our secret is a well-seasoned cast-iron plancha over a fiercely hot fire. And of course wild chanterelles presented three different ways.

Nutmeg-Pickled Chanterelles
Wild chanterelles have a particular sweetness and spiced flavour reminiscent of apricots and almonds. They are particularly delicious scented with nutmeg.

Makes 2 cups (500 mL)

1 cup (250 mL) cider vinegar
¼ cup (60 mL) pure liquid honey
1 tablespoon (15 mL) black peppercorns
2 teaspoons (10 mL) freshly grated nutmeg
1 teaspoon (5 mL) sea salt
1 pound (450 g) fresh chanterelle mushrooms,
    cleaned and trimmed

Measure the cider vinegar, honey, peppercorns, nutmeg, and salt into a medium saucepan. Bring to a boil over medium-high heat. Add the mushrooms and return to the boil. Transfer to a 2-cup (500 mL) mason jar or other storage container. Seal tightly and refrigerate for a month or so. Alternatively, process with careful canning procedures until shelf-stable.

recipe continues

Serves 8

PREP AND PLAN
- Make the Nutmeg-Pickled Chanterelles up to a month before you need them.
- On game day, gather all your ingredients, then prep each recipe, one by one, cleaning and tidying every tool as you go.
- Make the Chanterelle, Lentil, and Single Malt Scotch Stew.
- Make the Brown Butter Sherry Chanterelle Purée.
- Toss together the Sea Vegetable Salad.
- Sear the halibut. Begin plating as the fish cooks.

Chanterelle, Lentil, and Single Malt Scotch Stew

Rich, earthy lentils and fruity, peppery chanterelles unexpectedly bridged by earthy, peaty single malt Scotch.

2 tablespoons (30 mL) butter, divided
1 large white or yellow onion, finely diced
4 garlic cloves, finely minced
1 cup (250 mL) green lentils
2½ cups (625 mL) water
½ cup (125 mL) single malt Scotch
4 ounces (115 g) fresh wild chanterelle, oyster, or cremini mushrooms, cleaned, trimmed, and halved
1 teaspoon (5 mL) sea salt
Freshly ground pepper

Melt 1 tablespoon (15 mL) of the butter in a medium saucepan over medium-high heat. Add the onion and garlic and cook until sizzling and fragrant, 1 to 2 minutes. Add the lentils, water, and Scotch. Bring to a slow, steady simmer. Cover tightly, reduce the heat, and simmer until the lentils are tender yet firm, 15 minutes. Remove from the heat and, without uncovering, rest another 10 minutes.

Meanwhile, melt the remaining 1 tablespoon (15 mL) butter in a medium sauté pan or skillet over medium-high heat. Add the chanterelles, season with salt and pepper, and sauté until tender and fragrant, 2 or 3 minutes. Remove from the heat.

When the lentils have rested, gently stir in the mushrooms. Keep warm.

Brown Butter Sherry Chanterelle Purée

This creamless purée highlights the fruity aromas of chanterelle mushrooms with rich, nutty brown butter, sweet sherry, and sharp sherry vinegar.

Makes 1½ cups (375 mL)

4 tablespoons (60 mL) butter
8 ounces (225 g) fresh chanterelle mushrooms, cleaned and trimmed
½ cup (125 mL) sweet sherry
1 tablespoon (15 mL) sherry vinegar
½ teaspoon (2 mL) nutmeg
½ teaspoon (2 mL) sea salt
Freshly ground pepper

Toss the butter into a large saucepan over medium-high heat. Swirl gently as it melts, foams, and eventually forms a flavourful brown sediment. Toss in the chanterelles, sherry, sherry vinegar, nutmeg, salt, and pepper. Stir, bringing to a full simmer for a minute. Transfer the contents to a high-speed blender and process until luxuriously smooth. Return to the saucepan and reserve.

Sea Vegetable Salad

The pleasing brininess and crisp textures of foraged sea vegetables balance the sweet, mild halibut and aromatic mushrooms.

A handful or two of various freshly foraged sea vegetables—such as sea sandwort, sea asparagus, sea lettuce, seaweed, Hana Tsunomata sea vegetables (see page 50)—or watercress
A few spoonfuls of Nutmeg-Pickled Chanterelles and their pickling juice
A splash of extra-virgin canola oil or extra-virgin olive oil

Lightly toss everything together. Reserve.

recipe continues

Iron-Seared Halibut

The trick to searing delicate halibut is to balance consistent and exact heat with thick portions—enough heat to sear the outside of the flesh and enough thickness to keep the inside from over-cooking.

8 skinless, boneless fresh halibut fillets (4 to
    5 ounces/115 to 140 g each)
Fine sea salt
Freshly ground pepper
A few splashes of clarified butter or safflower or
    grapeseed oil

Generously season the fish with salt and pepper. Preheat a large cast-iron skillet, plancha, griddle, or non-stick pan over medium-high heat to precisely 425°F (220°C). For best results, use a surface thermometer. Splash a puddle of clarified butter into the pan. Carefully position the fillets in the oil. Patiently brown and crisp the bottom, 2 or 3 minutes, adjusting the heat as needed to maintain a steady sizzle. Carefully turn and cook until the bottom is brown and crisp and the fish is safely done, 2 to 3 minutes. An instant-read thermometer inserted in the thickest part should read 145°F (63°C). Rest briefly on paper towel, then plate immediately.

PLATE AND PRESENTATION
Fried sage leaves
Fresh sage sprigs
Ground sumac

- Curve a spoonful of the Brown Butter Sherry Chanterelle Purée around the middle of each plate.
- Place the Iron-Seared Halibut on the plate slightly overlapping the chanterelle purée.
- Spoon the Chanterelle, Lentil, and Single Malt Scotch Stew over the exposed purée.
- Top the fish with a tangle of the Sea Vegetable Salad and Nutmeg-Pickled Chanterelles.
- Place a few fried sage leaves among the lentils.
- Garnish with a fresh sage sprig.
- Add a bright red sprinkle of acidic ground wild sumac.

THIS YEAR'S LOBSTER AND LAST YEAR'S TURNIPS

ISLAND STYLE TAILS 'N' CLAWS, LOBSTER TAILS STUFFED WITH FERMENTED AND PICKLED TURNIP SLAW, TURNIP STEAKS, LOBSTER ROE TURNIP SAUCE, WATERCRESS PURÉE, FIRE-KISSED BEACH PEA SHOOTS

Our kitchen is mere moments from the Fortune wharf where each year our local fishing fleet ties up for the brief lobster season. Only during May and June is the season open on our end of the island, so during that time we honour the hard work of our fisherfolk every day. Lobster happily anchors our fish course when we open in mid-May and we sadly bid it farewell at the beginning of July as we move on to many other fish for the rest of the year.

Early in our growing season at the inn, with limited fresh options, we've found the humble storage turnip to be an ideal culinary companion. Its sweet texture and subtle earthy flavour give the root vegetable a surprising depth of flavourful possibilities, including a co-starring role in one of our signature sauces.

Island Style Tails 'n' Claws
A full lobster for each guest, classically poached in boiling seawater, then plunged in cold seawater and served chilled.

Serves 8, 1 lobster per person

8 live she-lobsters (1 to 1¼ pounds/450 to 565 g each)
Seawater (see page 127) or sea salt
A few pounds of ice cubes

Fill the largest pot you can muster three-quarters full of freshly foraged seawater. Alternatively, fill the pot with hot tap water, adding 1.3 ounces (35 g) of sea salt per quart (litre). Fill a second large pot or pail with more cold seawater and lots of ice cubes.

Pick up a lobster and grasp the claws firmly with your two hands. Cross them and with one hand hold them tightly together at the knuckles, under the claws. With your other hand, tug and slide the rubber bands off the claws. Immediately plunge the lobster into the boiling water.

Serves 8

PREP AND PLAN
- A few weeks or so in advance make the Fermented Turnip Slaw.
- A day or two in advance make the Pickled Turnip Slaw and Campari Onions.
- Poach and chill the lobsters the day before.
- On game day, gather all your ingredients, then prep each recipe, one at a time, cleaning and tidying every tool as you go.
- Prep the lobsters, breaking them down into tails, claws, knuckles, and roe, reserving the tail sections for the plate.
- Slowly roast the Turnip Steaks.
- Make the Lobster Roe Turnip Sauce. Reheat at the last minute.
- Make the Watercress Purée.
- Make the Liquid Sunshine Dressing and toss together the turnip slaw and stuff the empty lobster tail half shells.
- Fire-kiss the pea shoots.

recipe continues

Repeat with the remaining lobsters. Quickly return the water to a boil and cook the lobsters for 10 minutes. Using tongs, remove the red lobsters from the water and immediately plunge them into cold seawater for a minute or two. Remove and drain. Refrigerate upside down for a few hours, even overnight. The meat will reabsorb its juices as it cools and its best sweet flavour emerges.

Break down the lobsters: Wear a pair of heavy-duty kitchen gloves to protect your hands. Firmly grasp each lobster, tail in one hand, upper body in the other, and twist apart. Rest each tail smooth (bottom) side up. Insert the point of a knife blade into the middle of the tail fan. Carefully and firmly slice downwards, halving the shell and the meat within. Remove the two tail meat halves. Carefully remove and reserve the lobster roe for the sauce—it will appear as red "coral." Reserve half of the tail pieces (8 in total). Neatly trim their torn ends, reserving the scrap meat. Roughly chop the remaining tail halves and reserve in a separate bowl with the scrap meat. With sturdy kitchen scissors, neatly trim each empty tail half shell. Rinse well, drain, and reserve all 16 shell pieces.

Break the knuckles away from the claws and cut open with the scissors. Add their meat to the chopped tail meat. Carefully tug the smaller pincher of each claw back and forth, releasing the shell and with practice leaving the meat attached to the larger claw, even tugging out the inner cartilage membrane. Firmly crack each large claw with the back of a heavy knife. Carefully release the claw meat in one piece. Ease out the hidden fan-shaped cartilage. Cut a small slit on the back of the claw if it helps, but with practice, you'll learn to keep each claw intact. Reserve the claw meat in a separate bowl. Tug the smooth carapace shell away from the body and discard. Reserve any further lobster roe. Keep all the lobster meat and roe covered and refrigerated.

Lobster Tails Stuffed with Fermented and Pickled Turnip Slaw

This triple-turnip slaw highlights the incredible versatility of turnips and like any great salad includes an intriguing array of flavours.

A heaping tablespoonful (18 mL) of Fermented Turnip Slaw (page 252)
A heaping tablespoonful (18 mL) of Pickled Turnip Slaw (page 252)
A heaping tablespoonful (18 mL) of coarsely shredded peeled raw turnip
2 tablespoons (30 mL) minced Campari Onions (page 201)
Petals separated from a handful of chive blossoms (or ¼ cup/60 mL thinly sliced chives)
Reserved scrap meat from 8 lobsters (chopped tails, knuckles, and scrap meat)
2 tablespoons (30 mL) Liquid Sunshine Dressing (page 121) or extra-virgin olive oil
2 tablespoons (30 mL) mayonnaise
Sea salt
8 reserved lobster tail half shells

In a large bowl, combine the fermented, pickled, and raw turnip, Campari onions, chive petals, lobster meat, liquid sunshine dressing, and mayonnaise. Sprinkle generously with salt and stir together gently. Evenly fill the lobster tail half shells with the turnip slaw. Refrigerate until ready to serve.

recipe continues

Turnip Steaks

With patience, the firm texture of a turnip softens and yields its natural sweetness. This simple method highlights the root vegetable's earthy flavours and smooth texture.

Makes 8 steaks

A few splashes of clarified butter or safflower or grapeseed oil
1 large turnip, peeled, trimmed, and cut into 8 thick wedges
Sea salt
Freshly ground pepper

Preheat a cast-iron skillet, non-stick skillet, griddle, or plancha over medium heat, adjusting the heat until the surface temperature reaches 325°F (160°C). For best results, use a surface thermometer. Lightly oil the pan. Season the turnip steaks on both sides with salt and pepper. Carefully place the turnip steaks in the skillet and cook, flipping once or twice, until evenly browned and tender, about 20 minutes in total. Serve immediately or reserve and serve warm.

Lobster Roe Turnip Sauce

Unlike gummy potato or rice, turnip breaks down into a luxuriously smooth purée. Whether you use the optional turnip juice or not, you'll find this sauce the perfect neutral base for rich, flavourful lobster roe to shine.

Makes about 2 cups (500 mL)

2 heaping cups (550 mL) diced peeled turnip (about 1 pound/450 g)
1 cup (250 mL) raw turnip juice or water
¼ cup (60 mL) dry sherry
2 tablespoons (30 mL) sherry vinegar or cider vinegar
1 teaspoon (5 mL) sea salt
Reserved roe of 8 lobsters (about 1 cup/250 mL)

Toss the turnips into a small pot with the turnip juice, sherry, sherry vinegar, and salt. Cover tightly and simmer until tender, about 15 minutes. Stir in the lobster roe and continue to simmer until it's uniformly red, a minute or so. Transfer to a high-speed blender. Process until luxuriously smooth. Pass through a fine-mesh strainer. Transfer the sauce to a squeeze bottle or a small bowl.

Watercress Purée

This purée adds a vivid splash of bright green and the peppery freshness of watercress to the mix.

Makes about 1 cup (250 mL)

1 large bunch of fresh watercress or arugula,
    reserving 8 sprigs for garnish
¼ cup (60 mL) extra-virgin olive oil

Fill a medium bowl with ice water. Bring a large pot of lightly salted water to a boil. Briefly plunge the watercress into the boiling water, swirling once or twice as it immediately brightens. Immediately drain the watercress and quickly plunge it into the ice water, swirling and cooling rapidly. Drain again and transfer to a high-speed blender with the olive oil. Process until smooth. If your blender struggles, add a splash or two of water. Taste and season with a pinch of salt, if needed. Remove every single bright drop and transfer to a squeeze bottle or small bowl.

Fire-Kissed Beach Pea Shoots

For a few brief weeks each year we forage tender, sweet beach pea shoots before they become tough storm-proof plants. They're sweet like the pea shoots on our farm but their texture is much stronger since they're wild plants. Unlike the tender shoots we grow, the ones we forage from various local beaches are hardy enough to weather a literal scorching in live flames. You'll need a roaring hardwood fire fitted with a fiercely hot grille, or alternatively you can scorch them over a gas grill or burner. You can also substitute farmed pea shoots and skip the fire.

A handful of freshly foraged beach pea shoots
Sea salt

Place the beach peas within the live flames of a fire. Quickly flip them once or twice as they scorch and darken here and there. Season with salt. Remove and place directly on the plate or reserve in a single layer on a baking sheet.

PLATE AND PRESENTATION
Reserved fresh watercress
Dried cured lobster roe or smoked paprika

- Place a Fire-Kissed Beach Pea Shoot on each plate.
- Creatively position on each plate a stuffed lobster tail, a chilled lobster tail half, two claws, and a turnip steak.
- Invert the 8 remaining tail half shells and arrange on each plate as a decorative element.
- Sauce the plates with a few generous spoonfuls or precise squirts of the Lobster Roe Turnip Sauce.
- Sauce with the Watercress Purée.
- Garnish with a sprig of fresh watercress and a sprinkle of grated dried cured lobster roe or smoked paprika.

WILD BLUEFIN TUNA, FENNEL, AND BASIL

IRON-SEARED TUNA TATAKI, FENNEL SEED AND BASIL SCENTED TUNA TARTARE, WHITE FENNEL PURÉE, GREEN FENNEL PURÉE, PICKLED FENNEL AND GARDEN BASIL SALAD

Of the many fish landed on our Island shores, perhaps none is as respected as the bluefin tuna. For many years, I've watched our fisherfolk land the fish the old-fashioned way, with a rod and reel. I've followed a fish to Japan and seen the reverence it's accorded. Here at home, we're blessed with a well-managed sustainable fishery, so I'm proud to support the hard work of the fishing community around me and serve this incredible treasure to our guests.

Pickled Fennel and Garden Basil Salad

Crisp, sweet fennel is easily pickled with fennel seeds. Fennel's mild anise flavour is brightened by similar flavours in basil.

1 fennel bulb, trimmed, halved, cored, and very thinly sliced lengthwise
1 cup (250 mL) white wine vinegar
⅓ cup (75 mL) water
⅓ cup (75 mL) anisette or other anise liqueur such as Sambuca, Pernod, or ouzo
⅓ cup (75 mL) sugar
2 tablespoons (30 mL) fennel seeds
1 teaspoon (5 mL) salt
A variety of fresh basil leaves (about 40 leaves)

Place the fennel in a medium bowl. Into a small saucepan, measure the white wine vinegar, water, liqueur, sugar, fennel seeds, and salt and bring to a slow, steady simmer. Pour over the fennel. Thoroughly toss. Refrigerate for an hour or so, even overnight, tossing occasionally. Just before serving, toss together with the basil leaves or arrange separately.

recipe continues

Serves 8

PREP AND PLAN
- Sharpen your best fish knife. You'll need it for the tataki.
- Make the Pickled Red Onions (page 253) for the Fennel Seed and Basil Scented Tuna Tartare the day before you need them.
- Pickle the fennel the day before you need it.
- On game day, gather all your ingredients, then prep each recipe, one at a time, cleaning and tidying as you go.
- Make the White Fennel Purée and Green Fennel Purée.
- Toss together the Pickled Fennel and Garden Basil Salad.
- Prep the Fennel Seed and Basil Scented Tuna Tartare. Finish just before serving.
- Prep and sear the tuna tataki.

White Fennel Purée

This purée highlights the pure anise-like flavour of a fennel bulb.

Makes about 2 cups (500 mL)

1 fennel bulb, trimmed, halved, cored, and diced
1 cup (250 mL) water
¼ cup (60 mL) extra-virgin olive oil
1 tablespoon (15 mL) white wine vinegar
1 tablespoon (15 mL) anisette or other anise
   liqueur such as Sambuca, Pernod, or ouzo
½ teaspoon (2 mL) sea salt
¼ cup (60 mL) fennel flowers, yellow tips pulled
   from green stems (optional)

Toss the fennel and water into a medium saucepan. Bring to a slow, steady simmer, cover tightly, and continue simmering until tender, 10 minutes or so. Transfer to a high-speed blender with the olive oil, white wine vinegar, liqueur, and salt. Add the fennel flowers, if using. Process until thoroughly puréed and luxuriously smooth. Transfer to a squeeze bottle or a small bowl.

Green Fennel Purée

This purée highlights the vibrant colour of fennel tops and their subtle anise-like flavour.

Makes about 1 cup (250 mL)

Fronds from 2 fennel bulbs
¼ cup (60 mL) extra-virgin olive oil

Fill a medium bowl with ice water. Bring a large pot of lightly salted water to a boil. Briefly plunge the fennel fronds into the boiling water, swirling once or twice as they immediately brighten. Immediately drain the fennel and plunge it into the ice water, swirling and cooling rapidly. Drain again and transfer to a blender with the olive oil. Process until smooth. If your blender struggles, add a splash or two of water. Remove every single bright drop and reserve in a squeeze bottle or small bowl.

Fennel Seed and Basil Scented Tuna Tartare

The prized fattiness of impeccably fresh tuna is best enjoyed chilled and raw. In this tartare the luxurious richness of the fish is balanced with the sweet crunch of the freshest garden beans, aromatic fennel seeds, and fragrant basil.

1 pound (450 g) sashimi-grade tuna
½ cup (125 mL) trimmed and thinly sliced yellow
   beans
½ cup (125 mL) trimmed and thinly sliced green
   beans
½ cup (125 mL) trimmed and thinly sliced purple
   beans
½ cup (125 mL) Pickled Red Onions (page 253),
   minced
1 jalapeño pepper, stemmed, seeded, rinsed,
   and finely minced
2 tablespoons (30 mL) or more fresh green
   fennel seeds or fennel flowers
12 large basil leaves, stacked, tightly rolled, and
   thinly sliced
2 tablespoons (30 mL) extra-virgin olive oil
1 teaspoon (5 mL) sea salt

Meticulously slice and dice the tuna into ¼-inch (5 mm) cubes. Place the cubes in a medium bowl and lay a piece of plastic wrap directly on the fish. Refrigerate until thoroughly chilled, at least an hour.

In a medium bowl, mix together all the beans, the pickled red onions, jalapeño, fennel seeds, and basil. Cover with plastic wrap and refrigerate until thoroughly chilled. Just before serving, gently stir in the diced tuna, olive oil, and salt. Serve immediately.

Iron-Seared Tuna Tataki

Tuna is delicious served raw, but equally delicious seared until crispy. Tataki offers the best of both worlds. The luscious fattiness of tuna and an intensely hot skillet help the surface sear quickly before the middle can overcook and dry out.

8 ounces (225 g) sashimi-grade tuna, cut into 2 x 2 x 4-inch (5 x 5 x 10 cm) pieces
Sea salt
A few splashes of safflower or grapeseed oil

Preheat a large cast-iron skillet, plancha, griddle, or non-stick skillet over medium-high heat to precisely 450°F (230°C). For best results, use a surface thermometer. Generously season the fish with salt.

Pour a thin film of safflower into the pan. Carefully add the tuna and quickly sear on all sides. Rest briefly on paper towel. With a sharp knife, slice into ¼-inch (5 mm) slices.

PLATE AND PRESENTATION
Fresh fennel flowers

- Stand a 1½-inch (4 cm) tall and 2¼-inch (5.7 cm) wide ring mould or a standard biscuit cutter in the centre of the first plate. Fill the mould with tuna tartare, pressing gently into place. Carefully remove the mould. Repeat with the remaining tartare on the remaining plates.
- Onto each plate, spoon a puddle of White Fennel Purée to one side of the tartare. Carefully spoon the Green Fennel Purée into the middle of that puddle.
- Position a small fan of basil leaves between the purée and tartare. Nestle a pile of Pickled Fennel and Garden Basil Salad on the basil leaves.
- Slice the tuna tataki. Position a slice or two on the pickled fennel.
- Garnish with a fresh fennel flower.

IRON-SEARED ISLAND SCALLOPS

BEET CAVIAR, PICKLED ROASTED LEEKS, BEET SAUCE, PUMPKIN CHIPS

On Prince Edward Island, the secret to our scallops is their world-class freshness. They go from the water to the plate in mere hours. Serving any fish the same day it's caught is a rare luxury that we never take for granted. Years ago as a young chef at the inn, the first time I cooked just-shucked scallops they were so fresh they were still quivering as I seasoned them. I was hooked then and still am. Thirty years later, I still love them seared golden brown and delicious.

Pickled Roasted Leeks

Leeks are sweet, and like their onion cousins they are delicious when caramelized. Their concentrated rings are also ideal for absorbing pickling liquid. This recipe combines roasting and pickling.

Makes 16 pickled leeks

1½ cups (375 mL) cider vinegar or sherry vinegar
½ cup (125 mL) water
1 cup (250 mL) sugar
1 tablespoon (15 mL) coriander seeds
1 tablespoon (15 mL) fennel seeds
2 bay leaves, broken into small pieces
1 teaspoon (5 mL) sea salt
A splash of clarified butter or safflower or grapeseed oil
1 large leek, top and bottom trimmed, cut into sixteen 1-inch
    (2.5 cm) coins

Into a small saucepan, measure the cider vinegar, water, sugar, coriander seeds, fennel seeds, bay leaves, and salt. Bring to a full boil over medium-high heat, then reduce the heat and simmer for 5 minutes.

Preheat a medium, heavy skillet over medium-high heat. Add the clarified butter and swirl into a thin film. Carefully add the leeks, cut side down. Sear until the bottom is thoroughly caramelized. Carefully transfer to the hot pickling juice. Gently simmer over medium heat for 5 minutes. Remove from the heat and reserve or refrigerate for up to 1 month.

recipe continues

Serves 8

PREP AND PLAN
- Make the Pickled Roasted Beets up to 1 month ahead.
- Make the Beet Caviar 1 or 2 days before needed.
- Make the Pumpkin Chips the day needed.
- On game day, gather all your ingredients, then prep each recipe, one at a time, cleaning and tidying as you go.
- Make the Beet Sauce.
- Sear the scallops.
- Finish and plate.

Beet Caviar

It's surprisingly easy to make your own caviar. After curing, the eggs are beautifully stained by fresh beet juice.

Makes 2 cups (500 mL)

1 full skein trout or salmon roe
4 cups (1 L) water
¼ cup (60 mL) sea salt
1 cup (250 mL) fresh beet juice

Carefully split the skein to create an opening for the eggs to emerge. Place a mesh cooling rack over a medium bowl. Place the skein egg side down on the rack and, without pressing hard, move the skein over the rack to ease the eggs through the rack into the bowl. Most will fall easily, and some will pop. Discard the membrane and any bits within the eggs. Stir together the water and salt in a 4-cup (1 L) mason jar or another medium bowl. Transfer the eggs to the brine. Cover tightly and refrigerate for 12 hours.

Drain well. Return the eggs to the jar or bowl and cover with the beet juice. Refrigerate so the juice is absorbed into the eggs, at least an hour. Use immediately or cover and refrigerate for up to 1 week.

Pumpkin Chips

Many types of squash are bred for long winter storage, so their juices tend to be very sweet and starchy. With patient dehydration, they dry into a mouth-watering crisp garnish.

Makes 8 large chips

2 cups (500 mL) fresh juice from 4 pounds (1.8 kg) or so of pumpkin, winter squash, butternut squash, or acorn squash
1 teaspoon (5 mL) sea salt

Preheat a dehydrator to 140°F (60°C). Line the dehydrator tray with a silicone baking mat or parchment paper. Season the squash juice with salt and pour onto the tray. Carefully transfer to the dehydrator. Dehydrate until evenly crisp, 4 to 6 hours. Break into large chips and store in a resealable plastic bag at room temperature for up to 1 week.

Beet Sauce

The rich earthiness of beets is complemented with layers of fragrant woodsy flavour and aromatic spices. An intriguingly flavoured and brightly balanced sauce.

Makes about 2 cups (500 mL)

1 cup (250 mL) red wine
2 tablespoons (30 mL) minced fresh rosemary
1 tablespoon (15 mL) juniper berries
1 teaspoon (5 mL) sea salt
½ teaspoon (2 mL) ground allspice
½ teaspoon (2 mL) ground cloves
2 ancho chilies, stems removed and broken into pieces
1 pound (450 g) beets, trimmed, peeled, and quartered
¼ cup (60 mL) balsamic vinegar
2 tablespoons (30 mL) extra-virgin olive oil
1 teaspoon (5 mL) pure vanilla extract

Into a large saucepan, measure the red wine, rosemary, juniper, salt, allspice, cloves, and chilies. Bring to a steady simmer over medium heat. Add the beets, cover tightly, reduce the heat, and slowly simmer until tender, about 15 minutes. Transfer to a high-speed blender with the balsamic vinegar, olive oil, and vanilla. Process until thoroughly puréed and luxuriously smooth. Transfer to a squeeze bottle or a small bowl.

Iron-Seared Island Scallops

Searing scallops is a race against time. Your goal is to caramelize the outside without overcooking the inside. The secret is large, fresh scallops and a preheated heavy skillet.

2 dozen large fresh scallops, resting on folded paper towels
Sea salt
Freshly ground pepper
A splash of clarified butter or safflower or grapeseed oil

Generously season the scallops with salt and pepper. Heat a large cast-iron skillet, plancha, griddle, or non-stick skillet over medium-high heat to precisely 450°F (230°C). For best results, use a surface thermometer. Add the clarified butter and swirl into a thin film. Working quickly, carefully add the scallops to the pan one at a time. Cook until golden brown and seared, 2 or 3 minutes. Turn and sear the other side. (For smaller scallops, skip the second sear so as not to overcook the scallops.) Transfer briefly to fresh paper towel to absorb excess oil, then plate.

PLATE AND PRESENTATION
Fresh microgreens

- Place a spoonful of Beet Sauce in the centre of a plate.
- Position 3 seared scallops to one side of the sauce.
- Add 2 leek rounds to the presentation.
- Top each scallop with a small spoonful of Beet Caviar.
- Add a few shards of Pumpkin Chips.
- Garnish with fresh microgreens.

Meat, Potatoes, and Vegetables

SMOKEHOUSE BRISKET

SPICED BARK

Of all the many meats that come and go from our smokehouse, none is as memorable or as difficult as beef brisket. Cooks all over the world have found far simpler ways to cook this particular cut of meat, but a patient day in the smokehouse transforms it like no other cooking method. Anyone who has spent any time smoking meat understands the challenge. We also understand intense cravings. Deep primal instincts are triggered by this full expression of our smokehouse's potential. Mastering smoked brisket is like earning a wood-fired PhD with an edible diploma!

As with all artisanal cooking methods, full flavour depends on many variables far beyond the black-and-white of words on a page. Each variable is merely a challenge, though, another opportunity for mastery. The grade, size, freshness, and moisture and fat content of a particular cut of meat, your smokehouse rig, how often you open it, the size of the fire, the moisture content in your wood, the ambient temperature, and wind and weather conditions all have an effect.

This signature blend of aromatic flavours is optimized to help form the crunchy "bark" so characteristic of smoked brisket.

Salt the Brisket
Generously season the entire brisket with salt, favouring the thicker end (called the point) with more salt than the thinner end (called the flat). Place on a baking sheet, cover tightly with plastic wrap, and refrigerate overnight.

Make the Spiced Bark
In a small bowl, whisk together the black pepper, rosemary, sugar, chili powder, paprika, star anise, onion powder, garlic powder, and dry mustard.

Smoke the Brisket
Build and tend an aromatic fire in your smokehouse. Alternatively, fire up your barbecue or grill. Position a full water pan between the heat source and the eventual meat. Stabilize the smoky heat between 225°F and 250°F (110°C to 120°C). Just before smoking the brisket, discard any accumulated juices, then sprinkle the spiced bark blend evenly over the meat. Patiently smoke the brisket until its internal

recipe continues

Serves 12

Special Equipment Needed:
backyard smokehouse, Big Green Egg, or enclosed outdoor grill; lots of slow-burning hardwood or aromatic fruitwood (such as apple or cherry); optional lump charcoal, hardwood chips, fruitwood chips, or cedar shavings; thermometer probe with a remote sensor; fire pit kit (page 11)

SMOKEHOUSE BRISKET
1 brisket (12 pounds/5.4 kg), fatty side trimmed to ¼ inch (5 mm)
¼ cup (60 mL) sea salt

SPICED BARK
2 tablespoons (30 mL) black pepper
1 tablespoon (15 mL) finely minced fresh rosemary
1 tablespoon (15 mL) sugar
1 tablespoon (15 mL) chipotle, ancho, or other chili powder
1 tablespoon (15 mL) smoked paprika
1 tablespoon (15 mL) ground star anise
1 tablespoon (15 mL) onion powder
1½ teaspoons (7 mL) garlic powder
1½ teaspoons (7 mL) dry mustard

Liquid Steak (page 164), for serving

temperature reaches 203°F (95°C), 12 hours or so. Monitor the temperature with a remote sensor. The temperature will slowly climb to 150°F (65°C) or so before stalling for hours and hours, but eventually it will continue climbing again. At 203°F (95°C), the meat's connective tissues pass a magical threshold and begin dissolving. Remove from the smokehouse. Wrap tightly in foil or butcher's paper and rest in a tightly sealed picnic cooler for texture-improving carryover cooking, 2 to 3 hours. The meat will slowly cool to 160°F (70°C) or so while reabsorbing moisture and relaxing its texture.

Unwrap, slice, and serve immediately as we do with a slice or two of tender grilled beef and lots of garden-fresh vegetables, all topped with a ladleful of liquid steak.

Serve with:
Whey-Poached Potatoes (page 176)

Cabbage Steaks (page 190) or Roasted Broccoli and Cauliflower (page 193)

SMOKEHOUSE PORK BELLY

MAPLE-BRINED, MAPLE-SMOKED

A quivering, juicy, meltingly tender pork belly is one of the holy grails of the smokehouse. It's what I was dreaming of years ago when I dared to sketch a basic design for my Mason buddy. It's been an obsession since we built our first fire. Today I'm proud that when the smokehouse door slams shut on pork night, I know that in six hours we'll be there. A smoky, sweet, succulent pork belly has become one of our smokehouse signatures. The secret? An overnight soak in maple syrup, then an all-day maplewood smoke. Maple and maple. Deliciously appropriate.

As with all artisanal cooking methods, full flavour depends on many variables far beyond the black-and-white of words on paper. Each variable is merely a challenge, though, another opportunity for mastery. The grade, size, freshness, and moisture and fat content of a particular cut of meat, your smokehouse rig, how often you open it, the size of the fire, the moisture content in your wood, the ambient temperature, and wind and weather conditions all have an effect.

Marinate the Pork Belly

Turn the pork belly fatty skin side up. With a sharp knife, evenly score the skin, forming a tight diamond pattern, making long parallel cuts about 1 inch (2.5 cm) apart and ½ inch (1 cm) deep, first one way, then the other. Flip over and evenly season with half of the salt and lots of pepper. Flip back over and repeat with the remaining salt and more pepper, bending the meat to expose the inside of the fat as you do. Rest the meat skin side up in a large pan. Slowly pour the maple syrup over the top of the meat, helping it find its way evenly into the nooks and crannies of the scored fat. Cover the pan with plastic wrap and refrigerate for 8 to 12 hours.

Smoke the Pork Belly

Build and tend an aromatic fire in your smokehouse. Alternatively, fire up your barbecue or grill. Position a full water pan between the heat source and the eventual meat. Stabilize the smoky heat between 225°F and 250°F (110°C to 120°C). Discard accumulated juices from the pork belly before smoking. Patiently smoke the pork belly until its internal temperature reaches 190°F (88°C), 6 hours or so. Monitor the temperature with a remote sensor. The temperature will slowly climb

recipe continues

Serves 12 or more

Special Equipment Needed:
backyard smokehouse or enclosed outdoor grill; lots of aromatic maple or other slow-burning hardwood or fruitwood (such as apple or cherry); optional lump charcoal, hardwood chips, fruitwood chips, or cedar shavings; thermometer probe with a remote sensor; fire pit kit (page 11)

1 whole pork belly (10 to 12 pounds/4.5 to 5.4 kg)
½ cup (125 mL) kosher salt (I use Morton)
Lots of freshly ground pepper
1 cup (250 mL) pure maple syrup

to the magical mark of 190°F (88°C), when the meat will be meltingly tender and juicy. Remove from the smokehouse. Wrap tightly in foil or butcher's paper and rest in a tightly sealed picnic cooler to slowly cool to 160°F (70°C) or so while reabsorbing moisture and relaxing the texture, 1 hour.

Unwrap, slice, and serve immediately as we do with a slice or two of grilled pork loin, lots of garden-fresh vegetables, and a ladleful of pork jus.

Serve with:
Grilled Gouda Polenta (page 186)

Baked Acorn Squash (page 202)

WOOD-GRILLED BUTCHER'S STEAK

STEAKHOUSE BUTTER

Every butcher knows that tender cuts of meat are easier to cook and thus worth more to their customers. That's why filet mignon is so expensive—and bland. In an old-fashioned meat shop, loin cuts were always sold at a premium price, so butchers took lesser cuts home to their families. Every butcher had a few private reserve cuts that they secretly knew were just as good as, if not better than, the pricy cuts in the display case. They knew how to find the richly marbled, deeply beefy flatiron steak deep in the shoulder. The secret is out, though, and now it's our favourite grilling cut at the inn, where we finish it with a luxurious ladleful of Liquid Steak (page 164). At home I prefer to top grilled steak with a slice of classic compound butter from a stash I always keep in my freezer. As it melts it mingles with the meat's juices, forming a tangy sauce of sorts.

Make the Steakhouse Butter

In a small bowl, stir together the butter, horseradish, shallots, garlic, anchovies, tarragon, lemon zest and juice, and pepper until well combined.

Lightly mist a work surface with spray oil. Lay an 18-inch (46 cm) piece of plastic wrap on the oiled surface. (The spray oil will help the plastic wrap adhere to the work surface.) Scoop the butter along one long edge, forming a log shape roughly 8 inches (20 cm) long. Roll the butter once so it is covered in the plastic wrap, press into shape, then tightly roll all the way. Grasp the ends of the plastic and twirl the works a few times to tighten the butter into a perfect round log. Refrigerate until the butter is firm enough to slice, 2 to 3 hours or overnight, or freeze.

Grill the Butcher's Steak

Two hours or so in advance of grilling, generously season the steaks with salt and pepper. Cover with plastic wrap and refrigerate.

Build and tend an aromatic fire in your firepit, burning down to a thick bed of glowing hot coals. Alternatively, fire up your barbecue or grill. Grill the steaks, turning them frequently, evenly caramelizing the exterior, and not bothering with perfect steakhouse grill marks. Continue

Serves 4 to 6

Special Equipment Needed:
backyard fire pit or enclosed outdoor grill; lots of slow-burning hardwood or aromatic fruitwood (such as apple or cherry); optional lump charcoal, hardwood chips, fruitwood chips, or cedar shavings; fire pit kit (page 11)

STEAKHOUSE BUTTER
(MAKES EXTRA)
1 pound (450 g) butter, softened
2 tablespoons (30 mL) prepared horseradish or Dijon mustard
4 shallots, finely minced
4 garlic cloves, finely minced
4 anchovy fillets, finely minced
½ cup (125 mL) fresh tarragon or parsley, finely minced
Zest and juice of 1 lemon
Lots of freshly ground pepper

WOOD-GRILLED BUTCHER'S STEAK
1 full flatiron steak (2 pounds/ 900 g), cut into 2 narrower steaks, tough inner fascia membrane trimmed
Sea salt
Freshly ground pepper
Liquid Steak (page 11), for serving (optional)

recipe continues

cooking until a thermometer reads 125°F (50°C). Rest for a few minutes before slicing.

Slice the steakhouse butter into ¼-inch (5 mm) rounds and rest at room temperature. Thinly slice the steaks across the grain. Serve with a slice of steakhouse butter oozingly melting on top of the steak, or a ladleful of liquid steak, or both.

Serve with:
Whey-Poached Potatoes (page 176) or Smoked Potato Purée (page 179)

Cabbage Steaks (page 190), Skillet-Roasted Brussels Sprouts (page 198), or Fire-Kissed Bok Choy (page 206)

LIQUID STEAK

This finishing jus is one of the most extravagant things we do in our kitchen. First, we craft a rich simmering broth of beef shanks, full-bodied red wine, aromatic vegetables, and fresh herbs. Then we reduce the works until a deeply beefy, luxuriously smooth jus emerges. Lastly, we ladle the results over even more beef. In essence, we dedicate the extra-beefy flavour from one cut to the service of another cut. Let's just say there are no leftovers in our stock pot.

Every night we finish our meat, potato, and vegetable course with a ladleful of a complementary jus. But only the richest, purest, beefiest broths in our kitchen earn the honourable distinction of "Liquid Steak," a badge of honour for the cook.

_____

Preheat the broiler.

Each beef shank is encircled with a tough outer membrane. Cut through that membrane in 2 or 3 places. Place a single layer of shanks in a large, heavy skillet or roasting pan. Broil, flipping occasionally, until both sides are evenly browned. Meaty juices will accumulate in the pan and eventually begin sizzling and browning. If they begin to blacken, add a splash of water to slow them down while the meat finishes.

Remove from the oven and carefully pour in half the bottle of wine. Rest a few minutes to dissolve and loosen the accumulated flavour bits. Transfer the shanks and all the liquid to a large pot, stirring and scraping in every last drop. Add the remaining ingredients and the remaining wine. Bring the works to a slow, steady simmer. Cover tightly and continue simmering for 2 hours. Remove from the heat and, without uncovering, rest for 1 hour.

Pour through a fine-mesh strainer into a saucepan, pressing to extract every drop of precious flavour. Discard the solids. Carefully skim off any fat that floats on the surface. Bring to a rapid simmer and cook until reduced to 2 cups (500 mL) or so. Taste and season with salt. Ladle extravagantly over any grilled beef, or reserve and reheat.

Makes about 2 cups (500 mL)

3 pounds (1.35 kg) cross-cut beef shanks

1 bottle (26 ounces/750 mL) of your favourite big red wine, such as Cabernet Sauvignon

1 can (28 ounces/796 mL) whole or diced tomatoes

1 large yellow onion, thinly sliced

1 large carrot, peeled and thinly sliced

1 stalk celery, thinly sliced

Cloves from 1 head of garlic, peeled

4 sprigs fresh thyme

2 sprigs fresh rosemary

2 bay leaves

Sea salt

Lots of freshly ground pepper

4 cups (1 L) water

WOOD-ROASTED CIDER-BRINED PORK LOIN

A feast is for sharing your very best—and lots of it. We always bring as many different flavours to the table as possible, so each evening's meat course is a duo of cuts. We always pair something slow from the smokehouse, like Smokehouse Pork Belly (page 159) or Smokehouse Brisket (page 155), with something fast from the hearth or wood oven, like Wood-Grilled Butcher's Steak (page 161). On pork night, we serve smoked bellies with wood-roasted loins and our signature four-step pork loin play. First, the wet-brine method adds savouriness, sweetness, and a hint of apple flavour. Second, we slowly render and crisp the fat cap of the loin over one fire then, third, give it a fierce finishing roast with another fire. Lastly, a rest. No wood oven in your kitchen? No worries. A cider-brined pork loin roasted in an oven is still a beautiful thing.

Marinate the Pork Loin

In a medium bowl, whisk together the apple cider, salt, brown sugar, cinnamon, allspice, and hot sauce. With a sharp knife, evenly score the fat cap, forming a tight diamond pattern, making parallel cuts about 1 inch (2.5 cm) apart, first one way, then the other. Place the pork loin in a small container or loaf pan. Pour the cider brine over the meat to submerge it, cover tightly, and refrigerate long enough for the seasoned brine to be drawn into the meat, 6 to 8 hours.

Roast the Pork Loin

Fire up your wood oven, banking a small crackling hardwood fire to one side. Alternatively, preheat the oven to 350°F (180°C). Turn on the convection fan if you have one. Remove the pork loin from the brine and pat dry with paper towel. Discard the brine. Place the pork loin scored side up in a medium roasting pan. Transfer to the oven and roast until tender. The pork is done when a thermometer registers at least 145°F (63°C) in the thickest part of the loin. Begin checking the temperature after an hour or so, and expect about 90 minutes total cooking time. Remove from the oven, loosely cover with a small piece of folded foil, and rest as the meat relaxes and reabsorbs its juices, 10 minutes or so, before serving.

Serves 4 to 6

Special Equipment Needed (optional):
backyard smokehouse or enclosed outdoor grill; lots of aromatic maple or other slow-burning hardwood or aromatic fruitwood (such as apple or cherry); optional lump charcoal; fire pit kit (page 11)

4 cups (1 L) fresh apple cider
¼ cup (60 mL) sea salt
¼ cup (60 mL) tightly packed brown sugar
1 tablespoon (15 mL) cinnamon
½ teaspoon (2 mL) ground allspice
1 tablespoon (15 mL) hot sauce
1 boneless pork loin roast (3 to 4 pounds/1.35 to 1.8 kg), fat cap trimmed to ¼ inch (5 mm)

Serve with:
Cabbage Steaks (page 190)

Curry-Glazed Sweet Potatoes (page 197)

SMOKEHOUSE RIBS FOR SECONDS

On pork night our meat course is a slab of our signature Smoke-house Pork Belly (page 159) with a slice of Wood-Roasted Cider-Brined Pork Loin (page 167), lots of farm-fresh vegetables, and a ladleful of succulent pork jus. It's a beautiful plate of food. But our chefs love cooking ribs too, so as a reward to our guests and a nose-to-tail homage to the beast, we then offer ribs as seconds. It's a tradition. As soon as we finish serving the meat course, the chefs work their way along our long communal tables taking a bow and sharing these ribs. Not a bad gig.

As with all artisanal cooking methods, full flavour depends on many variables far beyond the black-and-white of words on paper. Each variable is merely a challenge, though, another opportunity for mastery. The grade, size, freshness, and moisture and fat content of a particular cut of meat, your smokehouse rig, how often you open it, the size of the fire, the moisture content in your wood, the ambient temperature, and wind and weather conditions all have an effect.

_____

Remove the shiny membrane from the curved underside of the ribs: tug or cut loose a corner, grasp firmly with paper towel, and peel it away.

In a small bowl, whisk together the brown sugar, paprika, onion powder, garlic powder, chili powder, and oregano. Lightly season the meaty side of the ribs with salt, then sprinkle evenly with the spice blend.

Build and tend an aromatic fire in your smokehouse. Alternatively, fire up your barbecue or grill. Position a water pan between the heat source and the eventual meat. Stabilize the smoky heat between 225°F and 250°F (110°C to 120°C). Patiently smoke the ribs until they're tender, 3 to 4 hours. You'll know they're done when you can grasp a protruding bone tip and gently twist it in place.

Serve with (for gatherings with finger food):
Staff Meal Chicken Wings (page 172)

Sunchoke Fries (page 205)

Bay Fortune Oyster Bar (page 79)

Serves 4 for dinner or
enough for a party

Special Equipment Needed:
backyard smokehouse or enclosed outdoor grill; lots of aromatic maple or other slow-burning hardwood or fruitwood (such as apple or cherry); optional lump charcoal, hardwood chips, fruitwood chips, or cedar shavings; thermometer probe with a remote sensor; fire pit kit (page 11)

4 racks back ribs, spareribs, or centre-cut ribs (about 10 pounds/4.5 kg in total)
2 tablespoons (30 mL) brown sugar
2 tablespoons (30 mL) sweet or smoked paprika
2 tablespoons (30 mL) onion powder
1 tablespoon (15 mL) garlic powder
1 tablespoon (15 mL) chipotle, ancho, or other chili powder
1 tablespoon (15 mL) dried oregano
Sea salt

WOOD-ROASTED SPATCHCOCK CHICKEN AND VEGETABLES

Few meals are as well suited for a wood oven as an old-fashioned roast chicken. And it's a classic: a chicken roasted on a bed of vegetables, then pulled apart, its juices and meat tossed into a roast stew of sorts. Delicious, and easily served.

Spatchcocking is a super-useful technique when you're in a hurry. Not only does it speed up the roasting time, but it also dramatically increases surface area, thus adding deep caramelized flavour. Street cred at the cooks' table. At your butcher's counter too: they'll be so thrilled you know the word "spatchcock," they'll happily do it for you.

___

Fire up your wood oven, banking a small crackling hardwood fire to one side. Intense heat and wood smoke are your aim, not flaming pizza heat with live flames licking across the ceiling. Alternatively, preheat the oven to 425°F (220°C). Turn on the convection fan if you have one. Preheat a large cast-iron skillet or roasting pan.

To spatchcock the chicken, lay it breast side down. With a pair of sharp kitchen shears cut along each side of the backbone, removing it and the attached neck. Turn the bird over and firmly press down on the breastbone and legs, flattening the bird as best you can. Season generously with salt and pepper.

Fill the preheated pan with the onions, garlic, lemon halves, and your chosen vegetables. Place the chicken, skin side up, on top. Return the pan to the oven and begin roasting. When the pan begins to sizzle, firmly shake it now and then to evenly coat the vegetables with flavourful juices. Continue cooking until the chicken is crispy, golden brown, and fragrant, up to an hour. The chicken is done when a thermometer registers at least 165°F (74°C) in the thickest part of the breast meat and thigh. Remove from the oven and rest. Share the crispy skin treat with all assembled. With a pair of tongs in each hand, pull, tug, and shred the meat away from the carcass. Sprinkle with fresh herbs and squeeze the roasted lemons with a pair of tongs, allowing the juices to mingle. Reserve the carcass for another day's chicken broth.

Serve with:
Tomato Marigold Salad (page 201), Summer Salad (page 216), or your favourite tangy green side salad

Serves 4 to 6

Special Equipment Needed (optional):
backyard smokehouse or enclosed outdoor grill; preheated wood oven, base fire and coal bed of fragrant hardwood or aromatic fruitwood (such as apple or cherry); optional lump charcoal; fire pit kit (page 11)

1 large roasting chicken (about 5 pounds/2.25 kg)
1 tablespoon (15 mL) fine sea salt
Lots of freshly ground pepper
4 white or yellow onions, peeled and quartered, keeping blossom end intact
Cloves from 1 head of garlic, peeled
2 lemons, cut in half
3 to 5 pounds (1.35 to 2.25 kg) assorted vegetables (such as potatoes, carrots, parsnips, turnips, sweet potatoes, beets, celery root, and celery stalks), peeled if necessary, cut into large bite-sized pieces
A handful of chopped aromatic fresh herbs, such as sage, thyme, rosemary, or tarragon

STAFF MEAL CHICKEN WINGS

MAPLE WHISKEY GLAZE

In most restaurants, chicken wings are tossed in the stock pot, if there's a stock pot at all. At the inn, we carefully keep all the wings for our cooks' afternoon family meal. Our guests enjoy the finer cuts while we suffer the leftovers. Or so the story goes. Truth is, we love chicken wings and don't mind getting our fingers messy one bit. Because wings are so versatile and we're so creative, everybody tries something different when it's their turn. We don't have a deep-fat fryer, so all our efforts are a wood-oven roast. This version was voted the best of the year by some very discerning palates.

Fire up your wood oven, banking a small crackling hardwood fire to one side. Alternatively, preheat the oven to 425°F (220°C). Turn on the convection fan if you have one. Ready a large cast-iron skillet. Alternatively, line 2 baking sheets with silicone baking mats or parchment paper.

In a large bowl, toss the wings with the vegetable oil, salt, and pepper. Fit the wings into the skillet or arrange on the baking sheets. Roast, occasionally stirring, until beautifully browned and tender, about 60 minutes.

Meanwhile, pour the maple syrup and whiskey into a small pot. Stir in the garlic and gently simmer over medium heat until the mixture reduces by two-thirds or so.

Transfer the chicken wings to a large bowl. Pour in the maple whiskey glaze. Toss gently until thoroughly coated. Sprinkle with the sesame seeds and minced fresh herbs. Toss lightly to combine. Serve immediately while steaming hot and crispy.

Serve with (for gatherings with finger food):
Smokehouse Ribs for Seconds (page 168)

Sunchoke Fries (page 205)

Bay Fortune Oyster Bar (page 79)

Serves 4

Special Equipment Needed (optional):
preheated wood oven, base fire and coal bed of fragrant hardwood or aromatic fruitwood (such as apple or cherry); fire pit kit (page 11)

24 whole chicken wings
2 tablespoons (30 mL) vegetable oil
1 tablespoon (15 mL) salt
1 tablespoon (15 mL) freshly ground pepper
1 cup (250 mL) pure maple syrup
½ cup (125 mL) Canadian whiskey
8 garlic cloves, thinly sliced
½ cup (125 mL) sesame seeds
A handful of fresh parsley sprigs, finely minced
Leaves from a few sprigs fresh thyme, minced

HASSELBACK POTATOES

GREEN CREAM

On Prince Edward Island we take our potatoes very seriously. Our kitchen is surrounded by farms and farmers working hard to grow the best spuds on the planet. The rhythm of their fields is part of the landscape of our lives. A simple baked potato honours their hard work, but sometimes you need to get dressed up for a special occasion. This Hasselback method is how our cooks show off a bit for their fellow cooks. We don't grow large baking potatoes on our farm—we bring them in from a local farm for our chowder—so this method is reserved for our staff meal. It's a bit more effort than just tossing some bakers in the oven, but it does honour the occasion. It also means someone is so efficient in their service prep that they have extra time for their mates. Very hospitable.

Preheat the oven to 400°F (200°C). Turn on the convection fan if you have one.

Roast the Hasselback Potatoes

Prep the potatoes one at a time. Cut a thin slice from one side of the potato so it rests firmly on the cutting board. Nestle a chopstick or thick skewer along each of the potato's long sides. Thinly slice the potato crosswise from end to end. The stick will prevent the cuts from going all the way through. Tuck the slices from 1 garlic clove into each potato. Drizzle with melted butter or fat of your choice. Sprinkle evenly with minced thyme, salt, and pepper. Place on a baking sheet and bake until tender and lightly browned, about 1 hour. After 30 minutes brush with more butter or fat. Test for doneness by poking with a skewer.

Make the Green Cream

In a high-speed blender, combine the spinach, dill, horseradish, water, and salt. Process until smooth, scraping down the sides as needed. Transfer to a small bowl and stir in the perpetual sour cream until smooth. Serve a dollop or two with each potato.

Serves 4

HASSELBACK POTATOES
4 large russet (baking) potatoes (about 2 pounds/900 g), scrubbed and dried
4 large garlic cloves, thinly sliced
¼ cup (60 mL) melted butter, olive oil, bacon drippings, or reserved duck, pork, beef, chicken, or turkey fat
Leaves from a few sprigs fresh thyme or rosemary, finely minced
1 teaspoon (5 mL) sea salt
Freshly ground pepper

GREEN CREAM
1 cup (250 mL) packed baby spinach leaves
1 cup (250 mL) fresh dill sprigs
¼ cup (60 mL) prepared horseradish
¼ cup (60 mL) water
¼ teaspoon (1 mL) sea salt
1 cup (250 mL) Perpetual Sour Cream (page 251) or store-bought

WHEY-POACHED POTATOES

The basic two-step technique used in this dish is found throughout the world of potatoes: slow, moist tenderizing followed by fast, dry crisping. But this dish is much more. The sustainable ideals that inspire our kitchen have led to a creative focus on lowering waste. Our cooks instinctively incorporate waste reduction into their practices. Cheesemakers all over the world stumbled onto this technique long ago. We save the whey from our daily fresh cheese production to pre-cook the specialty potatoes from our farm. As they simmer tender in the leftover liquid, they absorb lots of sweet, tangy flavour. They're ideally poised for a crispy roasting, perhaps even flavoured with a bit of reserved animal fat. Think of this dish as a tasty reminder that we can find many sustainable practices in the past that are still relevant today.

Preheat the oven to 400°F (200°C). Turn on the convection fan if you have one.

In a large saucepan, cover the potatoes with the whey and bring to a slow, steady simmer. Cook until tender, about 30 minutes. If you prefer more crispy edges, simmer the potatoes even longer until they are soft. Drain and transfer to a large, heavy skillet or roasting pan. Toss with a splash or two of the oil or fat of your choice. Season with salt. Roast until crispy, stirring or shaking occasionally, about 30 minutes. You'll find firmer potatoes will retain their shape, whereas softer potatoes will collapse and crisp even more.

Serves 6 to 8

2 to 3 pounds (900 g to 1.35 kg) small or baby potatoes
8 cups (2 L) fresh whey, whole milk, buttermilk, or water
¼ cup (60 mL) vegetable oil, olive oil, bacon drippings, or reserved duck, pork, beef, chicken, or turkey fat
Sea salt

SMOKED POTATO PURÉE

Wood-fire cooks are endlessly fascinated by the particular flavours of a specific wood's smoke. On Prince Edward Island we love maple, birch, and cedar and avoid the spruce, fir, and pine around us. But those smoky flavours are often tangled up with other flavours like spices, herbs, meats, and fish. The neutral flavour of this simple potato purée is an ideal way to carry the nuances of a particular wood smoke.

Build and tend an aromatic fire in your smokehouse. Alternatively, fire up your barbecue or grill. Stabilize the smoky heat between 225°F and 250°F (110°C to 120°C). Pour the cream into a shallow pan. Set the pan in the smokehouse and smoke the liquid until fragrant, an hour or so.

Meanwhile, set up a steamer basket in a large pot filled with about an inch of simmering water. Steam the potatoes until they are tender, 15 to 20 minutes. Pass through a ricer into a bowl. (Alternatively, press with a rubber spatula through a large sieve.) Bring the smoked cream to a simmer in a medium saucepan over low heat. Season with salt. Transfer the potatoes to the cream and stir vigorously into a smooth purée.

Serves 4 to 6

Special Equipment Needed: backyard smokehouse or enclosed outdoor grill; lots of slow-burning hardwood or aromatic fruitwood (such as apple or cherry); optional lump charcoal, hardwood chips, fruitwood chips, or cedar shavings; thermometer probe with a remote sensor; fire pit kit (page 11)

2 cups (500 mL) heavy (35%) cream
2 pounds (900 g) Yukon Gold or russet potatoes, peeled and cut into large cubes
1 teaspoon (5 mL) sea salt

BLUE RIBBON LOBSTER POTATO SALAD

If you're a chef on Prince Edward Island, why are you the one they always ask to bring the potato salad to the picnic? Because everybody knows you'll add lobster to the works. Try it yourself and you'll never go back to the plain old salad. Lobster and potatoes are a marriage made in heaven brought back to earth. It's also how you win potluck. Humble extravagance. "It's just some lobster." And a top-secret dressing loaded with bright garlic, tangy lemon, aromatic fresh herbs, and the real secret: a whole can of savoury anchovies.

Start the Salad
Bring a large pot of salted water to a rolling boil. Carefully add the potatoes. Return to the boil and continue cooking until the potatoes are tender, 10 minutes or so. Drain, then spread in a single layer on a baking sheet to quickly cool.

Meanwhile, Make the Dressing
To a blender or food processor, add the anchovies and their oil, olive oil, mustard, hot sauce, lemon zest and juice, and garlic. Purée until smooth.

In a large bowl, combine the cooled potatoes, lobster, carrots, celery, parsley, and dill. Add the dressing and thoroughly toss.

Serves 6 to 8

SALAD
3 pounds (1.35 kg) russet or
  Yukon Gold potatoes,
  scrubbed, cut into bite-sized
  pieces
The meat from 2 or 3 lobsters,
  chopped (see page 139)
2 carrots, peeled and shredded
2 stalks celery, finely diced
The tender leaves from a bunch
  of fresh parsley
The tender leaves from a bunch
  of fresh dill

DRESSING
1 can (2 ounces/50 g)
  anchovies
½ cup (125 mL) extra-virgin
  olive oil
1 tablespoon (15 mL) Dijon
  mustard
1 teaspoon (5 mL) hot sauce
Zest and juice of 2 lemons
Cloves from 1 head of garlic,
  peeled

POTATO BACON CHEDDAR TART

I created this signature dish for my very first menu at the Inn at Bay Fortune when I arrived on Prince Edward Island in 1992. It was an immediate hit and stayed on the menu for my entire seven-year tenure. I didn't stop making it when I moved on from the inn. After a few appearances on my various TV shows, it became an even bigger hit. Years later, a big-time food website in the States stumbled onto it, and it blew up into a massive viral hit. Even today it's still the single most popular recipe on my various websites. So after thirty years, I can confidently say this is my most popular recipe.

_____

Preheat the oven to 350°F (180°C). Turn on the convection fan if you have one.

Have ready a 10-inch (25 cm) or 12-inch (30 cm) non-stick sauté pan. Arrange the bacon slices in a radial pattern from the centre of the pan, up and over the sides. To reduce the thickness of the bacon in the centre, stagger every other slice, starting them 2 inches (5 cm) from the centre. The edges of the slices should overlap slightly as you work your way around the rim of the pan. With the palm of your hand, gently flatten the centre area. Season the works with lots of pepper.

Using a mandoline or sharp knife, evenly cut the potatoes into ¼ -inch (5 mm) slices. Lay a circular pattern of overlapping slices around the inside bottom edge of the pan. Continue layering the potatoes until the bottom is evenly covered. Season with salt and pepper. Sprinkle with fresh thyme. Sprinkle on a thin, even layer of grated cheese, barely enough to hide the potatoes below. Continue alternating layers of the potatoes, seasoning, and cheese until the pan is full, ending with a layer of potatoes and gently pressing as you go. Add two more layers, each inset an inch or so from the previous layer. The top should be higher than the pan's rim. Working your way around the pan, neatly fold the overhanging bacon up and over the potatoes. Place a small ovenproof plate on the bacon to prevent the ends from shrinking back during cooking.

Place the sauté pan on a baking sheet to contain bubbling juices. Bake until tender, about 3 hours. It's done when you can easily pierce it with a thin-bladed knife. Pressing with the plate to steady the tart, pour off the fat around the edges. Cover with a cutting board and carefully invert. Remove the pan and let rest for 10 minutes or so before slicing into wedges.

Serves 8

2 pounds (900 g) bacon
Freshly ground pepper
5 or 6 large baking potatoes, scrubbed
Sea salt
1 tablespoon (15 mL) minced fresh thyme
12 ounces (340 g) medium aged cheddar, coarsely grated

BROWN BUTTER POTATO GNOCCHI

FALL MUSHROOM BROTH

Around the world there are many ways to make a batch of tender gnocchi. Here on Prince Edward Island, since potatoes and mushrooms arrive together in the fall, this has become my favourite way to make these little dumplings. Potato dough simmered tender, crisped in brown butter, finished with a rich mushroom broth. In the Maritimes we're blessed with a wide variety of mushrooms both cultivated and wild-foraged, and we have the wild foragers to go get them.

Make the Mushroom Broth

Toss the butter into a large, heavy skillet over medium-high heat. Swirl gently as it melts, foams, and eventually lightly browns. Add the mushrooms and sauté until they release moisture and eventually begin to lightly brown, 10 minutes or so. Add the sherry and simmer until the liquid reduces by half. Add the broth, sage, thyme, sherry vinegar, and salt. Simmer for a minute, then remove from the heat. Taste and adjust seasoning. Reserve, keeping warm. Briefly return to a simmer just before serving.

Make the Potato Gnocchi

Place the potatoes in a large pot and cover with salted water. Bring to a boil over medium-high heat and boil until tender, 15 minutes or so. Drain the potatoes, rinse the pot, fill with hot water, and return to a simmer. Pass the potatoes through a ricer or food mill fitted with its finest disc into a large bowl and let cool, 15 minutes or so. Once the steam stops, sprinkle in 1½ cups (375 mL) of the flour. Add the eggs, nutmeg, salt, and pepper. Vigorously stir the mixture into a rough dough with a sturdy wooden spoon.

Measure the remaining ½ cup (125 mL) flour onto a work surface. Lightly flour your hands and the work surface, reserving some flour to the side. Turn out the dough and lightly sprinkle with the reserved flour. Knead for a minute until a smooth dough emerges. Divide the dough into 4 pieces. Dust one with flour and roll into a long, even rope about 1 inch (2.5 cm) thick. Repeat with the remaining 3 pieces. Cut each rope into 1-inch (2.5 cm) pieces. You should have 32 gnocchi.

Serves 4

FALL MUSHROOM BROTH
4 tablespoons (60 mL) butter
1 pound (450 g) assorted
    foraged wild mushrooms
    (such as chanterelle, porcini,
    matsutake, hen-of-the-woods,
    shiitake, oyster), tougher
    stems trimmed away, rinsed
    in running water, well
    drained, and thinly sliced
1 cup (250 mL) sweet sherry
4 cups (1 L) chicken, turkey,
    pork, beef, or vegetable
    broth
1 tablespoon (15 mL) thinly
    sliced fresh sage
1 tablespoon (15 mL) finely
    minced fresh thyme
1 tablespoon (15 mL) sherry
    vinegar
½ teaspoon (2 mL) sea salt
Freshly ground pepper

POTATO GNOCCHI
4 large russet or Yukon Gold
    potatoes (about 2 pounds/
    900 g), peeled and quartered
2 cups (500 mL) all-purpose
    flour, divided
2 eggs, whisked
1 teaspoon (5 mL) nutmeg
1 teaspoon (5 mL) sea salt
4 tablespoons (60 mL) butter

Bring the simmering water to a boil over medium-high heat. Working quickly and carefully, immediately transfer the dough pieces to the boiling water. Cook, stirring gently, until all the gnocchi are floating and cooked through, 3 to 4 minutes. Remove from the heat.

Melt the butter in a large non-stick skillet over medium-high heat. With a skimmer or slotted spoon, lift the cooked gnocchi from the hot water, draining thoroughly, and transfer to the butter. Without stirring, patiently cook the gnocchi until just one side is thoroughly browned and crispy. (Meanwhile, briefly return the mushroom broth to a simmer.) Transfer the gnocchi to a large serving bowl for sharing or divide between individual bowls. Serve with a ladleful of hot mushroom broth.

GRILLED GOUDA POLENTA

Prince Edward Island is blessed with some of the finest dairy herds on the planet and a long tradition of cheese-making and appreciative chefs. Thirty years ago at the inn, one sous-chef in particular took pride in our local cheese board. He was also a polenta master. Today, after a storied chef's career, Jeff McCourt has become an award-winning artisanal cheesemaker specializing in flavoured Gouda (and fresh cheese curds, but that's another story). Every time I stir one of Glasgow Glen Farm's many varieties into a batch of polenta, I think of my buddy the cheesemaker. His smoked Gouda is my favourite, though. Its rich smokiness naturally complements the wood-driven cooking of the FireWorks at the inn. Jeff is still a big part of our kitchen.

We often serve grilled polenta as part of a vegetarian presentation or as a side to various meat and fish dishes.

Lightly oil an 8 x 4-inch (1.5 L) or 9 x 5-inch (2 L) loaf pan.

Heat the vegetable oil in a large saucepan over medium-high heat. Add the onion and garlic and sauté until they soften and fragrant, 2 or 3 minutes. Pour in the broth. Season with salt and pepper. Briefly bring to a furious boil, then reduce the heat to a slow, steady simmer. Whisking constantly to prevent lumps, slowly pour in the cornmeal. Switch to a wooden spoon and continue simmering, stirring frequently, until the cornmeal absorbs all the liquid and a thick, smooth polenta forms, 10 minutes or so. Add the cheese a handful at a time, stirring until fully incorporated before adding more. Scrape the polenta into the loaf pan and smooth the top. Cover with plastic wrap. Refrigerate until cold and firm, at least 1 to 2 hours or overnight.

Turn the polenta out of the loaf pan and cut into 12 thick, even slices. Lay the slices close together on a baking sheet. Lightly moisten with spray oil.

Build and tend an aromatic fire in your backyard. Alternatively, fire up your barbecue or grill. Firmly position a grille over the fire. Carefully position the polenta slices on the grate and grill, turning once or twice, until evenly and lightly browned. (Alternatively, melt the butter in a large non-stick or cast-iron skillet over medium heat. Patiently brown each polenta slice, 2 or 3 minutes per side.)

Serves 4 to 6, makes 12 slices

Special Equipment Needed:
backyard fire pit or enclosed outdoor grill or barbecue; base fire and coal bed of fragrant hardwood (such as maple, birch, oak, or hickory) or aromatic fruitwood (such as apple or cherry); fire pit kit (page 11)

1 tablespoon (15 mL) vegetable or olive oil
1 large yellow onion, finely diced
4 garlic cloves, minced
4 cups (1 L) chicken broth, vegetable broth, or water
½ teaspoon (1 mL) salt
Lots of freshly ground pepper
1 cup (250 mL) polenta cornmeal or other coarsely ground cornmeal
8 ounces (225 g) Gouda cheese or your favourite cheese, shredded
4 tablespoons (60 mL) butter or vegetable oil, for optional stovetop cooking

RED FIFE PORRIDGE

SAGE WALNUT GOAT CHEESE PESTO

The whole wheat grain is known as the wheat berry. It is usually turned into flour. But instead of removing the bran and grinding it into powder, you can also treat it like other grains and cook it whole. Barley, millet, oats, quinoa, rice, rye, and spelt are all cooked whole, so why not wheat? We prefer the Red Fife varietal we grow on Prince Edward Island, but with patient cooking any wheat berry becomes chewy-tender and great tasting. As it soaks and simmers it releases starches that thicken the broth into a sauce of sorts that easily absorbs the bright, distinctive flavours of the pesto. You can enjoy this porridge on its own or pair with any meat or fish.

Start the Red Fife Porridge
Soak the wheat berries in water overnight to help them fully hydrate and soften.

Make the Sage Walnut Goat Cheese Pesto
Preheat the oven to 350°F (180°C). Line a baking sheet with parchment paper.

Spread the walnuts on the prepared baking sheet and toast for 10 minutes or so to brighten their flavour. Let cool.

In a food processor, combine the garlic, canola oil, sage, salt, and walnuts. Process into a smooth purée, scraping down the sides once or twice. Add the cheese and process until smooth. Reserve.

Finish the Red Fife Porridge
Melt the butter in a large saucepan over medium-high heat. Add the onion and garlic and sauté until lightly browned and fragrant, 5 minutes or so. Add the wheat berries (discard their soaking water) and the broth. Add the bay leaf and season with salt and pepper. Bring to a slow, steady simmer. Cover tightly, adjust the heat to the lowest setting, and continue cooking until the wheat berries are softened, about 1 hour. Serve a ladleful of the warm porridge with a dollop of sage walnut goat cheese pesto on top.

Serves 4 to 6

RED FIFE PORRIDGE
1 cup (250 mL) Red Fife wheat berries or other variety
2 tablespoons (30 mL) butter
1 large yellow onion, finely diced
4 garlic cloves, finely minced
4 cups (1 L) vegetable broth, chicken broth, or water
1 bay leaf
1 teaspoon (5 mL) sea salt
Freshly ground pepper

SAGE WALNUT
GOAT CHEESE PESTO
1 cup (250 mL) walnut pieces or halves, toasted
2 garlic cloves
2 tablespoons (30 mL) extra-virgin canola oil or extra-virgin olive oil
Leaves from 1 bunch fresh sage (about 1 cup/250 mL)
½ teaspoon (2 mL) sea salt
2 ounces (55 g) soft goat cheese

CABBAGE STEAKS

ROSEMARY JUNIPER APPLE JAM

Cabbage's reputation as a crisp anchor for the coleslaws of the world is well deserved, but it's not a one-trick pony. Like so many other foods, cabbage benefits from slow, patient heat—the only sort of heat that leads to deep golden caramelization.

In a slow cooker, apples readily absorb aromatic herb and spice flavours while softening into bright, luscious jam. Make the jam a day or two before you need it.

Make the Rosemary Juniper Apple Jam

In a slow cooker, stir together the brown sugar, red wine, and apple cider vinegar.

Place the juniper berries and bay leaves in a small square of cheese-cloth. Gather together the corners, forming a small sack, and tie closed with kitchen string. Nestle the bag into the wine mixture with the rosemary, then cover with the apples. Cook at the highest setting for 8 hours. The apples will soften and collapse, thickening the mixture and deepening its flavour. (Alternatively, place all the ingredients in a tightly covered casserole dish and bake in the oven at 250°F/120°C for 6 hours.) Fish out the bag of spices and discard. Leave the rosemary leaves in the mixture. Purée until smooth with an immersion blender or in a food processor. Transfer to a storage jar, cover tightly, and refrigerate for up to 2 weeks.

Make the Cabbage Steaks

Carefully cut the cabbage through the stem, first in half, then into quarters. Evenly season the cut faces of the cabbage with salt and pepper.

Heat a large cast-iron skillet, plancha, griddle, or non-stick skillet over medium-high heat to precisely 350°F (180°C). For best results, use a surface thermometer. Add the safflower oil to the pan. Position the cabbage wedges in the pan so a cut side is in full contact with the cooking surface. If you're using a skillet, tightly cover it. Cook, turning occasionally, as the cabbage gently sizzles and lightly caramelizes. Eventually the steamy moisture will work its way into the middle and tenderize it, 30 minutes or so. Serve the cabbage wedges with a dollop of the rosemary juniper apple jam.

Serves 4

ROSEMARY JUNIPER APPLE JAM (MAKES EXTRA)
1 cup (250 mL) tightly packed brown sugar
2 cups (500 mL) red wine
1 tablespoon (15 mL) apple cider vinegar or red wine vinegar
¼ cup (60 mL) juniper berries
2 bay leaves
Leaves from 8 sprigs fresh rosemary
5 pounds (2.25 kg) apples (Honeycrisp, McIntosh, Cortland, Jonagold, or Granny Smith), unpeeled, cored and quartered

CABBAGE STEAKS
1 green cabbage
Sea salt
Freshly ground pepper
A few splashes of safflower oil, grapeseed oil, clarified butter, or other reserved animal fat (see page 10)

ROASTED BROCCOLI AND CAULIFLOWER

CHICKEN SKIN GREMOLATA

Broccoli and cauliflower sometimes have a rather dull reputation. So it's easy to exceed expectations when you treat them with a bit of excitement. Like fierce heat. Roasting releases deliciously caramelized flavours from the sweet vegetables. Sprinkling on a bright and crunchy gremolata infused with the best part of a chicken doesn't hurt either. It's an extravagant way to make a condiment, but that's what happens when the same person grows and cooks the vegetable. Respect for your ingredients can elevate the humblest vegetable to a starring role with a brand-new colourful reputation.

Make the Chicken Skin Gremolata

Preheat the oven to 325°F (160°C). Turn on the convection fan if you have one. Line a baking sheet with a silicone baking mat or parchment paper. Lightly mist with spray oil.

Lay the chicken skin in a single layer on the prepared baking sheet, tugging and snipping as needed to flatten the skin. Season with poultry seasoning, salt (if needed), and pepper. Cover with another baking mat or parchment paper. Lay another baking sheet on top and flatten firmly. Add the weight of a pot or pan or two and bake until golden brown, rendered, and crispy, an hour or so. Remove from the oven. Increase the heat to 450°F (230°C).

Remove the top pan and baking mat or parchment. Rest the skin until cooled. Break up the skin and transfer with at least 2 tablespoons (30 mL) of the rendered fat to a food processor. Add the parsley, garlic, and lemon zest and juice. Pulse briefly, scraping down the sides once or twice, until the mixture is coarsely ground and evenly combined.

Make the Roasted Broccoli and Cauliflower

Trim the stems off the broccoli. Cut the broccoli lengthwise through its stem into 5 or 6 long spears. Trim out the core from the cauliflower and cut into large florets. Transfer the broccoli and cauliflower to a roasting pan or baking sheet and toss with the vegetable oil. Season with salt and pepper. Roast until caramelized, slightly charred, and tender, stirring once, 20 minutes or so. Transfer to a platter and sprinkle with the chicken skin gremolata.

Serves 6 to 8

CHICKEN SKIN GREMOLATA
The skin of a chicken (find a good soup pot for the rest of the chicken)
1 teaspoon (5 mL) poultry seasoning
1 teaspoon (5 mL) sea salt (only if poultry seasoning is sodium-free)
Freshly ground pepper
Leaves from 1 bunch fresh flat-leaf parsley
2 garlic cloves, minced
Zest of 2 lemons
Juice of 1 lemon

ROASTED BROCCOLI AND CAULIFLOWER
1 bunch broccoli
1 head cauliflower
¼ cup (60 mL) vegetable oil, olive oil, bacon drippings, or reserved duck, pork, beef, chicken, or turkey fat
1 teaspoon (5 mL) sea salt
Freshly ground pepper

JUNE HODGEPODGE

Hodgepodge is an institution in the Maritimes. Traditionally made with the first fresh vegetables of the season, it's an annual dish of hope after a long, cold winter and a spring of warming anticipation. Perhaps that ritual explains its legendary status. Of course, as with all the great dishes of the world, it's also seasoned with fierce debates over authenticity. Various traditional versions have legitimately evolved, but certain things are standard. It needs to be more soup than stew. New potatoes, yellow beans, peas, and milk (cream for guests) are essential. And arguments. I don't mind when people argue about vegetables, though. They all agree this is a delicious dish any time of the year.

Toss the butter into a large pot over medium heat. Add the onion and stir until sizzling and aromatic, a few minutes. Add the potatoes and carrots and pour in the milk and water. Season with salt and pepper. Bring to a slow, steady simmer, then reduce the heat and continue cooking until the potatoes are tender, 15 minutes or so. Pour off half the liquid and add the cream to the pot. Add the yellow beans, green beans, peas, turnips, squash, and fresh herb of choice. Simmer until beans and squash are tender, 10 minutes or so.

Serves 6 to 8

¼ cup (60 mL) butter
1 large yellow onion, finely minced
1 pound (450 g) baby new potatoes, quartered
1 large carrot, peeled and sliced
2 cups (500 mL) whole milk
2 cups (500 mL) water
1 tablespoon (15 mL) sea salt
Lots of freshly ground pepper
1 cup (250 mL) heavy (35%) cream
A handful of yellow beans, trimmed and cut in half crosswise
A handful of green beans, trimmed and cut in half crosswise
A handful of green peas
A handful of baby turnips, stem trimmed
A handful of pattypan squash, stem trimmed
A handful of fresh parsley, thyme, savory, tarragon, or dill, finely minced

CURRY-GLAZED SWEET POTATOES

PUMPKIN SEED PESTO

The intense sweetness of a sweet potato complements its intense nutritional density. Mother Nature may be trying to tempt us with candy to get us on our vitamins, but it's worth it. As sweet potato bakes, its sweetness intensifies and a deeper earthy flavour emerges. Here, that richness is then brightened and balanced with a finishing glaze of spiced honey vinegar. This is my favourite way to cook a sweet potato and one of my all-time favourite vegetable dishes. Especially when it's topped with an equally pedigreed pesto crafted with pumpkin seeds.

Make the Pumpkin Seed Pesto
Measure the pumpkin seeds, cheese, garlic, basil, lemon zest and juice, and pumpkin seed oil into a food processor. Purée until a smooth pesto emerges, scraping down the sides a few times along the way. Season with salt and reserve.

Make the Curry-Glazed Sweet Potatoes
Preheat the oven to 400°F (200°C). Turn on the convection fan if you have one.

Use the point of a small sharp knife to lightly score the surface of the sweet potatoes in a diamond pattern, making cuts ½ inch (1 cm) deep at ½-inch (1 cm) intervals. Arrange the sweet potatoes cut side up on a baking sheet and lightly oil the tops. Season with salt. Bake for 45 minutes or so.

Meanwhile, in a small bowl, stir together the honey, cider vinegar, hot sauce, and curry powder. Evenly spoon and smear the glaze all over the oven-hot potatoes. Continue baking until the sweet potatoes are glazed and tender, 15 minutes more. Serve with a generous dollop of pumpkin seed pesto on top.

Serves 4

PUMPKIN SEED PESTO
(MAKES EXTRA)
1 cup (250 mL) unsalted roasted pumpkin seeds
4 ounces (115 g) Parmigiano-Reggiano cheese, grated (½ cup/125 mL)
4 garlic cloves
Leaves from 2 bunches of fresh basil, cilantro, or flat-leaf parsley (about 2 cups/500 mL)
Zest and juice of 2 lemons
½ cup (125 mL) pumpkin seed oil or extra-virgin olive oil
Sea salt

CURRY-GLAZED SWEET POTATOES
2 large sweet potatoes, sliced in half lengthwise
2 tablespoons (30 mL) vegetable oil, olive oil, bacon drippings, or reserved duck, pork, beef, chicken, or turkey fat
½ teaspoon (2 mL) sea salt
2 tablespoons (30 mL) pure liquid honey
1 tablespoon (15 mL) cider vinegar
1 teaspoon (5 mL) hot sauce
1 tablespoon (15 mL) curry powder

SKILLET-ROASTED BRUSSELS SPROUTS

PANCETTA DRESSING

By a twist of fate, Brussels sprouts are perhaps the best vegetables for roasting. These miniature cabbages of sorts are loaded with sweetness and bright green flavour. You just have to know how to unlock it. Normally, high-heat roasting damages green vegetables, but not these little nuggets. Their tough overlapping leaves allow heat to caramelize their exterior without damaging their delicate green centre. High heat is the key for perfectly roasted veggies.

Preheat the oven to 450°F (230°C). Turn on the convection fan if you have one.

Make the Pancetta Dressing

Toss the pancetta into a small skillet over low heat and slowly cook, stirring frequently, until lightly browned, rendered, and crispy, about 15 minutes. Using a slotted spoon, strain out the crisp pancetta, leaving behind its fat. Reserve the pancetta. Add the sherry vinegar, honey, and mustard to the pan and bring to a full simmer. Remove from the heat and whisk until smooth. Reserve.

Make the Skillet-Roasted Brussels Sprouts

Toss the Brussels sprouts into a large, heavy skillet or roasting pan. Add the vegetable oil and season with salt and pepper. Toss everything together to evenly coat. Roast, stirring once or twice, until lightly browned and tender, 20 minutes or so. Add the pancetta dressing, toss to combine, and continue roasting as the sprouts absorb the dressing and glaze, 2 or 3 minutes longer. Serve with crisp pancetta bits sprinkled on top.

Serves 4 to 6

PANCETTA DRESSING
6 ounces (170 g) thinly sliced pancetta or bacon, cut into thin strips
¼ cup (60 mL) sherry vinegar
1 tablespoon (15 mL) pure liquid honey
1 tablespoon (15 mL) Dijon mustard

SKILLET-ROASTED BRUSSELS SPROUTS
2 pounds (900 g) Brussels sprouts, stems trimmed and loose or dry leaves removed
3 to 4 tablespoons (45 to 60 mL) vegetable oil, olive oil, bacon drippings, or reserved duck, pork, beef, chicken, or turkey fat
½ teaspoon (2 mL) sea salt
Freshly ground pepper

TOMATO MARIGOLD SALAD

CAMPARI ONIONS

Of the hundreds of fruits and vegetables we nurture on our farm, perhaps none is heralded and revered as much as the tomato. In our annual pursuit of warm-from-the-sun, vine-ripe flavour, we grow many, many types. Tomatoes are so essential in our kitchen that with so many variables on our biodynamic farm, we hedge our bets with variety. As the season comes and goes so do many individual types. One thing never changes, though: in every long row of tomatoes, every other plant is a fragrant marigold bush. Their perfume annoys the heck out of various pests, so our tomatoes are pest-free. We've also discovered that marigolds are beyond edible—they're delicious. Their bright multicoloured flowers have a light, sweet fragrance, while their tender frond-like leaves have a deeper herbaceous flavour. It's only natural that ripe tomatoes and marigolds are a perfect pairing. It's also epically validating for our farm.

Pickle the onions the day before you need them. You'll find the pleasingly bitter flavour of the Campari pairs well with the tart, sweet tomatoes.

Make the Campari Onions

Measure the red wine vinegar, sugar, and Campari into a medium saucepan. Bring to a full boil over medium heat. Gently stir in the red onions. Cover tightly, remove from the heat, and let sit at room temperature until cool, 1 to 2 hours. Cover and refrigerate overnight. They will last up to a month.

Make the Vinaigrette

Into a 2-cup (500 mL) mason jar, measure the shallots, sherry vinegar, liquid sunshine dressing, honey, mustard, salt, and pepper. Tightly screw on the lid and vigorously shake into a smooth dressing. Reserve until ready to serve or store overnight in the fridge. Shake before serving.

Make the Tomato Marigold Salad

Slice and dice the tomatoes into smaller bite-sized pieces. Transfer to a medium bowl. Lightly season with salt and pepper. Drizzle evenly with the vinaigrette. Top with a tangle or two of Campari onions. Sprinkle with the marigold leaves and flowers.

Serves 4 to 6

CAMPARI ONIONS
1 cup (250 mL) red wine vinegar
½ cup (125 mL) sugar
½ cup (125 mL) Campari
2 or 3 red onions, sliced into thin rings

VINAIGRETTE
2 shallots, very finely minced
¼ cup (60 mL) sherry vinegar or apple cider vinegar
¼ cup (60 mL) Liquid Sunshine Dressing (page 121) or extra-virgin olive oil
1 tablespoon (15 mL) pure liquid honey
1 teaspoon (5 mL) Dijon mustard
½ teaspoon (2 mL) sea salt
Lots of freshly ground pepper

TOMATO MARIGOLD SALAD
5 pounds (2.25 kg) ripe seasonal tomatoes
Sea salt
Freshly ground pepper
1 cup (250 mL) freshly picked marigold leaves
1 cup (250 mL) freshly picked marigold flowers

BAKED ACORN SQUASH

CARAWAY APPLESAUCE, RYE CRUST

Crack open an acorn squash and you'll reveal an inner hollow that's just begging to be stuffed full of flavour and tenderly baked. Over the years I've tried lots of filling ideas, mostly successfully. Let's just say hummus was not a hit. But applesauce always works; no matter how outlandish the flavours I can't resist adding to it. The mysteriously familiar caraway in this version adds a savoury note to the apples. The same spice inspires the complementary crispy rye crust. Winter squash, apples, and caraway. Magic.

Preheat the oven to 350°F (180°C). Turn on the convection fan if you have one.

Make the Caraway Applesauce
In a large saucepan, stir together the apples, brown sugar, rum, vanilla, and caraway seeds. Cook over medium-high heat, stirring occasionally, until the apples soften and collapse, 10 minutes or so. Purée until smooth with an immersion blender or in a food processor.

Make the Rye Crust
Break the toast slices into your food processor. Add the butter and caraway seeds and process into coarse crumbs.

Bake the Acorn Squash
Lightly oil the exposed flesh of the squash halves. Nestle the squash in a baking dish or on a baking sheet. Season with salt and pepper. Spoon the caraway applesauce into the squash halves, filling each cavity. Evenly sprinkle the rye crust mixture over the applesauce and exposed squash. Bake until lightly browned and tender, an hour or so.

Serves 4

CARAWAY APPLESAUCE
4 apples (Honeycrisp, McIntosh, Cortland, Jonagold, or Granny Smith), unpeeled, cored and chopped
½ cup (125 mL) tightly packed brown sugar
½ cup (125 mL) spiced rum
½ teaspoon (2 mL) pure vanilla extract
1 tablespoon (15 mL) caraway seeds

RYE CRUST
2 slices of rye bread, toasted
2 tablespoons (30 mL) butter, softened or melted
1 teaspoon (5 mL) caraway seeds

BAKED ACORN SQUASH
2 acorn squash, stemmed, cut in half lengthwise, and seeded
A splash or two of vegetable oil, olive oil, bacon drippings, or other reserved animal fat (see page 10)
Sea salt
Freshly ground pepper

SUNCHOKE FRIES

GREEN GODDESS DRESSING

Overwintered sunchokes (see page 15) have many distinctive characteristics, but the way they come alive in a deep-fryer is perhaps their best. These humble tubers are the very best vegetable for frying, and that's saying a lot on Prince Edward Island, where the mighty french fry reigns supreme. Sunchoke fries surpass potatoes with their impossible deliciousness. Imagine the crispiest, crunchiest crust possible revealing the tenderest sweet, creamy centre. Fry up a batch of sunchoke fries and I bet you'll love them as much as we do at the inn. For even more next-level flavour, fry them in rendered duck fat! They are especially tasty dipped in a fresh batch of classically bright and tangy green goddess dressing.

Make the Green Goddess Dressing

In a high-speed blender, combine the vegetable oil, lemon zest and juice, anchovies, garlic, watercress, tarragon, chives, and salt. Purée until bright green and smooth. In a medium bowl, whisk together the mayonnaise, perpetual sour cream, and green purée. Transfer to a storage jar, cover tightly, and refrigerate for up to 1 week.

Deep-Fry the Sunchokes

Heat the frying fat in a large pot or deep-fryer over medium heat until it reaches 375°F (190°C) on a deep-fat thermometer. Carefully add about half of the sunchokes, taking care not to crowd the hot oil and lower its temperature too far. Adjust the heat to maintain the ideal frying temperature of 365°F (185°C). Fry until they are golden brown and crispy, 5 minutes or so. Using a skimmer or slotted spoon, remove the fries from the hot oil and drain on paper towel. Season generously with salt and pepper. Repeat with the remaining sunchokes. Serve with green goddess dressing for dipping. Carefully cool, strain, and refrigerate the frying fat so you can use it again.

Serves 4 to 6

GREEN GODDESS DRESSING
¼ cup (60 mL) vegetable oil
Zest and juice of 1 lemon
4 anchovy fillets
2 garlic cloves
A handful of fresh watercress or
  baby spinach leaves
A handful of fresh tarragon
  leaves and tender stems
A handful of fresh chives (or the
  tops from 4 green onions),
  chopped
½ teaspoon (2 mL) sea salt
½ cup (125 mL) mayonnaise
½ cup (125 mL) Perpetual Sour
  Cream (page 251) or
  store-bought

SUNCHOKE FRIES
8 cups (2 L) lard, peanut oil,
  grapeseed oil, or rendered
  duck fat, for deep-frying
  (I prefer duck fat)
2 to 3 pounds (900 g to
  1.35 kg) sunchokes, washed,
  well drained, and halved
  lengthwise
Sea salt
Lots of freshly ground pepper

FIRE-KISSED BOK CHOY

CHARRED ROMESCO SAUCE

The holy grail of all green-vegetable cookery is to add real flavour without overcooking and damaging the vitality of the veggie. On the hearth you can reliably steam and sauté. You can also daringly fire-kiss. With the intense searing heat of a live flame and your hard-earned wood fire experience, you can master this flavourful method. The secret is a crackling wood fire that so quickly sears leafy greens that they don't have a chance to wilt. You'll sacrifice a few tasty charred tips for the greater good, but with care you'll easily judge the done-ness of the greens. Baby bok choy is ideally sized for the flame. Romesco sauce is a tangy Spanish classic and the perfect condiment with its balance of bright and charred flavours.

Make the Charred Romesco Sauce

Preheat the oven to 400°F (200°C).

Place the head of garlic in a small baking dish and roast for 45 minutes.

Meanwhile, build and tend an aromatic fire in your fireplace or back-yard, burning down to a thick bed of glowing hot coals. Alternatively, fire up your barbecue or grill to its highest setting. If cooking indoors, fire up your broiler.

Grill, roast, or broil the bell pepper and tomatoes until lightly charred, 15 minutes or so. Immediately transfer the pepper halves to a small bowl and cover with a plate or plastic wrap. Let steam until cool enough to handle, then peel away as much of the charred black skin as you can.

Transfer the bell pepper and tomatoes to a food processor or high-speed blender. Slice off the top third of the garlic head with a ser-rated knife to expose the cloves, then carefully squeeze the garlic cloves out of their skins and into the food processor. Drain the soaked chilies, remove their stems, and add along with the almonds, sherry vinegar, paprika, salt, and olive oil. Process to a chunky paste. Reserve.

Serves 4 to 6

Special Equipment Needed: backyard fire pit or enclosed outdoor grill; lots of slow-burning hardwood, aromatic fruitwood (such as apple or cherry), or lump charcoal; fire pit kit (page 11)

CHARRED ROMESCO SAUCE
1 head of garlic
1 red bell pepper, cut in half lengthwise, stem and seeds removed
4 Roma or plum tomatoes, halved lengthwise
2 dried ñora or ancho chilies, soaked in boiling water for 15 minutes
½ cup (125 mL) unsalted roasted almonds
2 tablespoons (30 mL) sherry vinegar
1 tablespoon (15 mL) smoked paprika
½ teaspoon (2 mL) salt
½ cup (125 mL) extra-virgin olive oil

FIRE-KISSED BOK CHOY
1 tablespoon (15 mL) vegetable oil
6 heads baby bok choy, gai lan, choy sum, or rapini, cut in half lengthwise
Sea salt

Grill the Bok Choy

Stoke the fire into a mass of live flame reaching through the grill grates. Evenly brush a small baking sheet with the vegetable oil. Dredge the cut side of each bok choy in the oil. A few at a time, carefully position the bok choy cut side down on the grill directly in the flames. Briefly sear—fire-kiss—until lightly charred, green and tender, just a minute or so. Season with salt. Repeat to grill the remaining bok choy. Serve with the charred romesco sauce.

SLOW ONIONS

GARLIC SCAPE AIOLI

Hidden within every onion is an incredibly rich golden-brown flavour that far transcends its initial raw sharpness. It's the onion's raison d'être. The secret to unlocking that deep flavour is time—culinary perseverance and a certain disciplined wait as time marches inexorably on. When it comes to onions, patience is an edible virtue. A virtue made even more appetizing with bright garlic scapes, the immature flower stalks that emerge from intentionally unharvested garlic on our farm. Their tender green version of garlic's familiar flavour is a revelation. We celebrate their fleeting season in this dish.

Make the Garlic Scape Aioli

Bring a small pot of lightly salted water to a boil. Chop 2 of the garlic scapes into 3 or 4 pieces each. Toss into the boiling water and cook for just a minute, long enough to heat through and brighten. Drain and cool under cold running water. Drain again. Transfer the garlic scapes to a high-speed blender and add the olive oil. Purée until smooth. Scrape every last drop into a small bowl. Reserve.

Add the garlic, egg yolks, water, and salt to the blender. Purée until smooth. Add the lemon zest and juice and blitz just to mix. Stir into the garlic scape purée, cover with plastic wrap, and refrigerate until ready to serve.

Make the Slow Onions

Preheat a large cast-iron, heavy-duty, or non-stick skillet over medium-low heat. Add the olive oil and swirl into an even film. Without disturbing their concentric rings, season the onions with salt and pepper. Snugly fill the pan with the onions cut side down. Cover tightly and patiently cook until the cut sides are beautifully caramelized, 30 minutes or so. Carefully turn and continue cooking until the onions are soft and the bottoms are lightly browned, 15 minutes or so. Transfer to a cutting board and cut into quarters. Transfer to a serving bowl.

Serves 4 to 6

Special Equipment Needed: backyard fire pit or enclosed outdoor grill; lots of slow-burning hardwood, aromatic fruitwood (such as apple or cherry), or lump charcoal; fire pit kit (page 11)

GARLIC SCAPE AIOLI
A handful of fresh garlic scapes or green onions, divided
1 cup (250 mL) extra-virgin olive oil
2 garlic cloves
2 egg yolks
2 tablespoons (30 mL) water
½ teaspoon (2 mL) sea salt
Zest and juice of 1 lemon

SLOW ONIONS
½ cup (125 mL) olive oil, vegetable oil, bacon drippings, or other reserved animal fat (see page 10)
4 to 6 large red or sweet onions, ends tightly trimmed, peeled, and cut in half crosswise
Sea salt
Lots of freshly ground pepper

Grill the Garlic Scapes

Build and tend an aromatic fire in your fireplace or backyard, burning down to a thick bed of glowing hot coals. Alternatively, fire up your barbecue or grill to its highest setting. If cooking indoors, fire up your broiler.

Toss the remaining garlic scapes with a splash of olive oil and season with salt and pepper. Grill until bright and tender, turning once or twice, just a few minutes.

Drizzle the onions with the garlic scape aioli and serve with the grilled garlic scapes.

WILTED KALE, CARROT, AND PARSNIP RIBBONS

SHALLOT DRESSING

This hearty vegetable salad is prepared in three steps. First, the veggies' strong earthy flavours are released with heat. Second, the flavours are locked in with cold. Lastly, they're balanced with a big, bright dressing. Kale, carrot, and parsnip are all excellent raw, but blanching them improves their texture, colour, and flavour. It is important to immediately plunge the steaming blanched veggies into icy cold water so they don't overcook or dull. The cold locks in their flavour so the dressing can bring it alive. The sweet, subtle pungency of shallots is also released by the dressing. You'll need a big bowl to contain all these flavours!

Make the Shallot Dressing

Measure the shallots, sherry vinegar, olive oil, mustard, honey, salt, and pepper into a 2-cup (500 mL) mason jar. Screw on the lid and shake until the contents emulsify into a smooth dressing. Refrigerate for up to a week.

Make the Wilted Kale, Carrot, and Parsnip Ribbons

Bring a large pot of salted water to a boil. Fill a large bowl with ice water. Briefly plunge the vegetables into the boiling water, swirling gently as they brighten and tenderize, just a minute or so. Immediately drain the vegetables and plunge them into the ice water, swirling and cooling them rapidly. Drain well. Transfer to a serving bowl, drizzle with the dressing, and toss to combine.

Serves 4 to 6

SHALLOT DRESSING
2 shallots, very finely minced
¼ cup (60 mL) sherry vinegar or cider vinegar
¼ cup (60 mL) extra-virgin olive oil
1 tablespoon (15 mL) Dijon mustard
1 tablespoon (15 mL) pure liquid honey
1 teaspoon (5 mL) sea salt
Lots of freshly ground pepper

WILTED KALE, CARROT, AND PARSNIP RIBBONS
5 or 6 large kale leaves (about 1 pound/450 g), centre rib cut out, rolled up and sliced ½ inch (1 cm) thick
1 large carrot, peeled into ribbons
1 large parsnip, peeled into ribbons

ROASTED CARROT, LENTIL, AND NASTURTIUM SALAD

NASTURTIUM HUMMUS

The surprisingly sharp, bright flavour of nasturtium leaves (see page 35) shines in this dish. They add a shocking green hue to the hummus and pack lots of snappy flavour. Save some leaves for the salad—they're one of our favourite greens and help define this dish. The flowers are equally delicious, though sweeter. Patient roasting brings out the rich, deep sweetness of carrots. Don't be deterred by a bit of black char or blistering. Carrots can withstand blackening without tasting burnt. For this one ingredient, blackness is a good sign.

Roast the Carrots

Preheat the oven to 425°F (220°C). Turn on the convection fan if you have one. Line a baking sheet with parchment paper.

Gently toss the carrots with the vegetable oil. Season with salt and pepper. Arrange the carrots in a single layer on the prepared baking sheet. Roast until tender and charred, 30 to 45 minutes, stirring once halfway through roasting.

Meanwhile, Make the Nasturtium Hummus

In a food processor, combine the tahini, lemon zest and juice, garlic, and olive oil. Purée until smooth. Add the chickpeas and process, scraping down the sides once or twice, until smooth. Add the nasturtium leaves and purée until smooth.

Assemble the Roasted Carrot, Lentil, and Nasturtium Salad

Arrange the roasted carrots in a bowl or on a platter. Top with the nasturtium hummus. Alternatively, smear the hummus on a platter and top with the carrots. Either way, top with the lentils and scatter nasturtium leaves and flowers on top.

Serves 4 to 6

ROASTED CARROT, LENTIL, AND NASTURTIUM SALAD
2 to 3 pounds (900 g to 1.35 kg) multicoloured carrot varieties (small carrots whole, larger carrots cut in half lengthwise)
¼ cup (60 mL) vegetable oil, olive oil, bacon drippings, or other reserved animal fat (see page 10)
Sea salt
Lots of freshly ground pepper
1 cup (250 mL) cooked red or green lentils
A handful each of fresh nasturtium leaves and flowers

NASTURTIUM HUMMUS
½ cup (125 mL) tahini
Zest and juice of 1 lemon
2 large garlic cloves
2 tablespoons (30 mL) extra-virgin olive oil
1 can (19 ounces/540 mL) chickpeas, drained and rinsed (about 1½ cups/375 mL)
4 ounces (115 g) fresh nasturtium leaves or baby spinach leaves, washed and drained

BABY TURNIPS

PINEAPPLE WEED PESTO

A freshly dug sixty-day turnip is a flavour revelation. Simply put, it's one of the most delicious vegetables we grow and hands down the best straight out of the ground raw. On our farm, they're practically begging to be pulled from the soil, their rounded tops visibly straining and emerging from below. Sweet, aromatic bliss with a bit of crisp crunch. They're worth waiting for, and so good as is that we prefer them raw, but a quick poach can improve the texture of a more mature crop.

You don't have to wander far from the turnip patch for condiment inspiration. Pineapple weed, also called wild chamomile, grows all along the fringes of our farm (and throughout North America). This perennial wild herb is named for its clear, distinct pineapple flavour. We brew fragrant tea with it and use it as a fresh herb in all sorts of dishes. Pineapple weed is best harvested when its distinctive flower pods are still tender and green, before they yellow and become bitter.

Make the Pineapple Weed Pesto

Toss the pineapple weed flowers, cashews, Parmesan, and garlic into a food processor. Process until coarsely chopped. With the machine still running, slowly pour in the liquid sunshine dressing and process until smooth. Season with salt. Refrigerate for up to a week.

Cook the Baby Turnips

Taste a turnip or two. If you find them a bit too firm or mature, bring a large pot of salted water to a boil. Fill a large bowl with ice water. Briefly plunge the turnips into the boiling water, swirling gently as they brighten and tenderize, just a minute or so. Immediately drain the turnips and plunge them into the ice water, swirling and cooling them rapidly. Drain well.

Transfer the turnips to a bowl. Season with salt and pepper. Top with the pineapple weed pesto and toss to combine. Garnish with a few pineapple weed flowers.

Serves 4 to 6

PINEAPPLE WEED PESTO
1 cup (250 mL) pineapple weed (wild chamomile) flowers, a few reserved for garnish
½ cup (125 mL) unsalted roasted cashews or almonds
½ cup (125 mL) grated Parmesan cheese
2 garlic cloves, chopped
½ cup (125 mL) Liquid Sunshine Dressing (page 121) or extra-virgin canola oil or olive oil
½ teaspoon (2 mL) sea salt

BABY TURNIPS
2 pounds (900 g) baby turnips
Sea salt
Freshly ground pepper

SUMMER SALAD

HERB DRESSING

There's a fleeting week every summer when at last everything seems to line up perfectly on our farm and in our herb garden. So much of farming is about waiting, so when the full harvest is finally upon us, when every row and every day brings another fresh flavour, we celebrate the best way we know how: with a vegetable-based salad with a simple dressing and the very best of our harvest. There's far more to this bowl and far more to the phrase "farm fresh" than mere words can convey. You can taste diversity, of course, since at the inn there're often more than fifty ingredients in the bowl. But you'll taste something more—a particular intensity of flavour that transcends even freshness. It's our own terroir, and it's become powerful enough to add real intensity to our farm's flavours. Nowhere is that more obvious than in a bowl of simple raw vegetables. Nowhere is that more celebrated.

Serves 8

HERB DRESSING
1 shallot, very finely minced
2 garlic cloves, very finely minced
¼ cup (60 mL) sherry vinegar or cider vinegar
¼ cup (60 mL) extra-virgin olive oil
1 tablespoon (30 mL) fresh fennel seeds, lovage pollen, or minced fresh tarragon
1 tablespoon (15 mL) Dijon mustard
1 tablespoon (15 mL) pure liquid honey
1 teaspoon (5 mL) sea salt
Lots of freshly ground pepper

SUMMER SALAD VEGETABLES
Farm-fresh vegetables, as many varieties as you can harvest and gather, a handful or so of each (2 to 3 pounds/900 g to 1.35 kg when prepped), such as
Tender fresh beans, trimmed
Multi-hued vine-ripened tomatoes, quartered
Baby squashes, trimmed and halved
Baby root vegetables (carrots, turnips, radishes), trimmed and halved
Sweet corn, trimmed from cob
Fresh peas, shucked
Snow peas
Snap peas
Fennel bulb, thinly sliced
Crisp cucumbers
Cucamelons, radish pods, and any other obscure varietals you can find

FRESH HERBS
Lots of freshly picked aromatic herb leaves, such as commonly available basil, mint, dill, chives, parsley, cilantro, and fennel fronds, and exotic specialty varieties, such as marigold, anise hyssop, lemon balm, nasturtium, shiso

EDIBLE FLOWERS
A handful or two of nasturtium, marigold, chive, borage, dill, fennel, arugula, broccoli, violet
A spoonful of Pickled Red Onions (page 253)

Make the Herb Dressing

Measure all the ingredients into a 2-cup (500 mL) mason jar. Screw on the lid and shake until the contents emulsify into a smooth dressing. Reserve.

Make the Summer Salad

Bring a large pot of salted water to a boil. Fill a large bowl with ice water.

As you prep the vegetables, sort them into two separate medium bowls: tougher-textured vegetables in one bowl (to blanch), tender vegetables in the second bowl (to be kept raw). Squashes, peas, fennel, and cucumbers are better left raw.

Tougher string beans, corn, and baby carrots or other roots benefit from blanching.

To blanch, briefly plunge the vegetables into the boiling water, swirling gently as they brighten and tenderize, just a minute or so. Immediately drain the vegetables and plunge them into the ice water, swirling and cooling them rapidly. Drain well and pat dry. Transfer to a large serving bowl.

Add the raw tender vegetables, herbs, and flowers. Drizzle with the herb dressing and toss to combine. Garnish with the pickled red onions.

Sweets and Treats

STRAWBERRY RHUBARB SHORTCAKE

NUTMEG BISCUITS, STRAWBERRY RHUBARB COMPOTE,
ROSE WHIPPED CREAM, PINK PEPPERCORN STRAWBERRY SORBET

On Prince Edward Island, strawberries are an eagerly anticipated seasonal treat, not a ubiquitously underripe and bland supermarket fruit. When you patiently await ripeness in the summer sun, your reward is intense, pure strawberry flavour. To honour the fruit, we pair it with traditional rhubarb and the complementary fragrance of rose petals foraged from my favourite wild rose bush. It's amazing how easily whipped cream absorbs the scent of rose petals, but since some roses are more fragrant than others, be sure to choose a strongly scented variety. Pink peppercorns add a bit of spicy balance and even more flowery aroma to a deeply flavoured sorbet that also highlights the true flavour of sun-ripe strawberries.

Pink Peppercorn Strawberry Sorbet

Fresh, ripe strawberry purée balanced with lemon and the floral fragrance and mild heat of pink peppercorns.

Makes about 6 cups (1.5 L)

2 quarts (2 L) hulled, fresh strawberries (2½ to 3 pounds/1.125 to 1.35 kg)
Juice of 1 lemon
2 tablespoons (30 mL) pink peppercorns
½ teaspoon (2 mL) sea salt
1 cup (250 mL) sugar

In a high-speed blender, purée a third or so of the strawberries with the lemon juice, pink peppercorns, and salt. Add the remaining strawberries and continue puréeing until smooth. Measure the purée. For each cup of purée, add ⅓ cup (75 mL) of sugar. Purée until smooth, then transfer to an ice-cream maker and process according to the manufacturer's instructions. Transfer to an airtight container and freeze until set, at least 4 hours. (Alternatively, transfer the purée to a shallow baking pan, cover tightly, and freeze until solid, 4 hours or overnight. Break the frozen purée into chunks, transfer to a food processor, and purée until smooth. Transfer to an airtight container and refreeze until firm, 2 hours.) Freeze for up to 1 month.

recipe continues

Serves 8

PREP AND PLAN
- Make the sorbet up to a month ahead.
- The biscuits can be made up to 5 days ahead if necessary and reheated.
- Infuse the Rose Whipped Cream a day or two in advance.
- Make the Strawberry Rhubarb Compote a day or two in advance.
- On the day, bake the biscuits, whip the cream, assemble the components, and present the dessert.

Rose Whipped Cream

Cream easily absorbs the fragrance of fresh roses and whips into a sublimely perfumed cloud.

Makes about 3 cups (750 mL)

2 cups (500 mL) heavy (35%) cream
Fragrant petals from 2 fresh roses
2 tablespoons (30 mL) sugar
1 teaspoon (5 mL) pure vanilla extract

Warm the cream to a bare simmer. Stir in the rose petals, transfer to a storage container, and refrigerate until thoroughly cold, at least 4 hours or overnight. Just before serving, strain out the rose petals, add the sugar and vanilla and whip until thick. Serve immediately or refrigerate for up to 1 hour.

Strawberry Rhubarb Compote

Tart rhubarb is balanced with sugar, then simmered soft. Local strawberries at the peak of seasonal perfection are added last to preserve their fresh flavour.

Makes about 8 cups (2 L)

1 pound (450 g) fresh rhubarb, cut into 1-inch
  (2.5 cm) chunks
1 cup (250 mL) sugar
½ cup (125 mL) water
3 pounds (1.35 kg) fresh strawberries, hulled and
  cut in half

Measure the rhubarb, sugar, and water into a large saucepan. Bring to a full boil over medium-high heat, stirring occasionally, then immediately reduce the heat to a slow, steady simmer. Cook until the rhubarb softens and breaks down, 10 minutes or so. Cool completely, then stir in the strawberries. Serve immediately or cover tightly and refrigerate for up to 3 days.

Nutmeg Biscuits

These nutmeg-scented dessert biscuits are easy to make, but it's their crunchy crust you'll remember.

Makes 12 biscuits

4 cups (1 L) all-purpose flour
¼ cup (60 mL) white sugar
2 tablespoons (30 mL) baking powder
1 tablespoon (15 mL) freshly grated nutmeg
¼ teaspoon (1 mL) sea salt
2½ cups (625 mL) heavy (35%) cream
1 teaspoon (5 mL) pure vanilla extract
2 tablespoons (30 mL) raw sugar
2 tablespoons (30 mL) fennel seeds
1 tablespoon (15 mL) any milk, for brushing

Preheat the oven to 425°F (220°C). Turn on the convection fan if you have one. Line a baking sheet with a silicone baking mat or parchment paper.

In a large bowl, whisk together the flour, white sugar, baking powder, nutmeg, and salt. Pour in the cream and vanilla. Using the handle of a wooden spoon, vigorously stir until a coarse dough forms. Lightly flour a work surface. Turn the dough out onto the work surface and knead a few times into a firm dough.

Pat the dough into an even disc about 1 inch (2.5 cm) thick. Cut into 12 even wedges and transfer to the prepared baking sheet, separating the wedges. Spread the raw sugar and fennel seeds on a small plate. Lightly brush the top of each biscuit with the milk, then pick up, invert, and carefully dip the sticky surface into the raw sugar, gently shaking off any excess before returning to the tray. Bake until golden brown, about 20 minutes. Cool on a rack. Store in a tightly sealed bag or container for up to 5 days before gently reheating.

PLATE AND PRESENTATION

- Cut a Nutmeg Biscuit in half. Position the bottom half of the biscuit on a plate.
- Layer a heaping spoonful or two of Strawberry Rhubarb Compote on the biscuit.
- Top with a large dollop of Rose Whipped Cream. Position the top half of the biscuit on top.
- Nestle a scoop of Pink Peppercorn Strawberry Sorbet next to the biscuit.

BROWN BUTTER RASPBERRY CAKES

RASPBERRY MINT COMPOTE, MULLED CABERNET RASPBERRY SAUCE, HONEY THYME FROZEN YOGURT, FENNEL SEED CRISP

While fresh raspberries are in season on Prince Edward Island, we feature them every night for dessert with a variety of methods and complementary flavours. This dish is one of our favourite ways to show off the versatility of the sweet-sour fruit. Baked and absorbed into a rich brown butter batter. Tossed into a simple last-second fresh compote with bright mint. Simmered into a richly flavoured sauce. Alongside the fresh-from-the-sun fruit are a tangy frozen treat scented with complementary fresh thyme and an intriguingly flavoured crisp spice cookie. Raspberries are deliciously inspirational.

Honey Thyme Frozen Yogurt
A smooth, creamy frozen treat with a tangy twist: full-fat yogurt and aromatic thyme.

Makes about 4 cups (1 L)

2 cups (500 mL) milk
1 cup (250 mL) sugar
2 tablespoons (30 mL) pure liquid honey
2 tablespoons (30 mL) finely minced fresh thyme leaves and tender
   stems
1 tablespoon (15 mL) pure vanilla extract
2 cups (500 mL) natural plain full-fat Greek yogurt

Measure the milk, sugar, honey, thyme, and vanilla into a medium saucepan. Stirring frequently, gently bring the mixture to a slow, steady simmer over medium heat. Remove from the heat, cover, and let sit until cool.

Measure the yogurt into a medium bowl and gently whisk in the milk mixture. Refrigerate until cold. Pour the cold yogurt mixture into an ice-cream maker and process according to the manufacturer's instructions. Transfer to an airtight container and freeze until set, at least 4 hours. Store for up to 1 week.

recipe continues

Serves 8

PREP AND PLAN
- A day or two in advance, make the frozen yogurt, raspberry sauce, and fennel seed crisp batter.
- On the day, bake the crisps, make the raspberry compote, bake the cakes, assemble the components, and present the dessert.

Mulled Cabernet Raspberry Sauce

Sweet-sour raspberries, complementary Cabernet Sauvignon, and aromatic spices richly flavour this easily made sauce.

Makes 2 cups (500 mL)

1 cup (500 mL) Cabernet Sauvignon
½ cup (125 mL) sugar
½ teaspoon (2 mL) ground allspice
¼ teaspoon (1 mL) ground cloves
Lots of freshly ground pepper
14 ounces (400 g) fresh or frozen raspberries
   (about 4 cups/1 L)

Measure the red wine, sugar, allspice, cloves, and pepper into a small saucepan. Bring to a slow, steady simmer over medium heat. Add the raspberries, return to a simmer, and continue cooking until the fruit is soft, 3 or 4 minutes. Transfer to a high-speed blender and purée until smooth. Strain through a fine-mesh strainer, pressing firmly with the back of a ladle or spoon to remove the seeds. Refrigerate for up to a week.

Fennel Seed Crisp

Licorice-flavoured fennel seeds in a classic lacy crisp.

Makes 12 crisps

4 tablespoons (60 mL) butter
¼ cup (60 mL) sugar
¼ cup (60 mL) corn syrup
¼ cup (60 mL) all-purpose flour
½ cup (125 mL) fennel seeds

Measure the butter, sugar, and corn syrup into a small saucepan. Whisk over medium heat until melted and smooth. Remove from the heat and whisk in the flour and fennel seeds. Transfer the batter to a covered container and refrigerate until firm, at least 1 hour or overnight.

Preheat the oven to 325°F (160°C). Line a baking sheet with lightly oiled parchment paper or a silicone baking mat.

Scoop 1 heaping tablespoon (18 mL) of the dough and shape into a ½-inch (1 cm) ball with your hands. Repeat, arranging the balls 3 inches (8 cm) apart on the prepared baking sheet. Bake until thin and evenly browned, 12 to 15 minutes. Cool on the baking sheet. Transfer crisps to an airtight container between layers of parchment paper. Store at room temperature for up to 3 days.

Raspberry Mint Compote

Fresh raspberries splashed with mint liqueur and tossed with fresh mint.

Makes 2 cups (500 mL)

8 ounces (225 g) fresh raspberries
1 ounce crème de menthe or peppermint
   schnapps
½ cup (125 mL) fresh mint leaves, stacked, tightly
   rolled, and thinly sliced into fine shreds

In a small bowl, gently toss together the raspberries, crème de menthe, and mint. Serve immediately or cover tightly and refrigerate for up to 2 days.

Brown Butter Raspberry Cakes

These richly flavoured cakes are infused with the richness of brown butter and studded with pockets of raspberries.

Makes 8 individual cakes

8 eggs
1 tablespoon (15 mL) pure vanilla extract
⅔ cup (150 mL) tightly packed brown sugar
1 teaspoon (5 mL) nutmeg
½ teaspoon (2 mL) sea salt
1 pound (450 g) butter
2 cups (500 mL) all-purpose flour
1 pound (450 g) fresh raspberries

Preheat the oven to 350°F (180°C). Turn on the convection fan if you have one. Lightly oil eight 6-ounce (175 mL) ramekins or other non-stick baking moulds. Sprinkle the moulds evenly with white sugar, shaking out any extra.

In a medium bowl, whisk together the eggs, vanilla, brown sugar, nutmeg, and salt. Toss the butter into a small saucepan over medium-high heat. Swirl gently as it melts, foams, and eventually forms a flavourful brown sediment. Immediately pour every drop (including the sediment) into the egg mixture, whisking constantly until smooth. Whisk in the flour until smooth.

Fill the ramekins about halfway with raspberries. Top with ½ cup (125 mL) or so of the batter. Bake until tender and golden brown, about 20 minutes. Rest for a few minutes, then invert onto plates and remove the ramekins. Serve immediately, or cool before storing at room temperature in a tightly sealed plastic bag for a few days, or freeze for up to 1 month.

PLATE AND PRESENTATION
Fresh mint sprigs

- Ladle a puddle of Mulled Cabernet Raspberry Sauce in the middle of each plate.
- Place a Brown Butter Raspberry Cake on top of the sauce.
- Top the cake with a spoonful of the Raspberry Mint Compote.
- Nestle a scoop of Honey Thyme Frozen Yogurt beside each cake.
- Garnish with a Fennel Seed Crisp and fresh mint sprigs.

ROSEMARY CARROT CAKES

PARSNIP CREAM CHEESE ICE CREAM, BEET PAINT, PUMPKIN SEED BRITTLE, CARROT RAISIN CHUTNEY

The classic carrot cake is so traditional on Prince Edward Island that there's always a hard-fought battle for bragging rights at every expo, agricultural fair, and bake sale. At the inn we respect that delicious tradition by baking a classic moist carrot cake, then surrounding it with familiar flavours. We can't resist mixing in a few twists, though. Rosemary replaces the familiar spices in the cake, those spices instead flavouring a carrot and raisin chutney. Cream cheese makes its expected appearance, this time in ice cream along with carrots' cousin parsnip. Fellow root vegetable beet appears in a sumptuously smooth sauce. And pumpkin seeds add seasonal crunch. Five-star carrot cake!

Parsnip Cream Cheese Ice Cream

The subtle earthiness of sweet parsnips and the richness of traditional cream cheese combine in this smooth ice cream.

Makes about 4 cups (1 L)

2 cups (500 mL) whole milk
2 cups (500 mL) peeled and shredded parsnips
2 cups (500 mL) cream cheese, at room temperature
¾ cup (175 mL) sugar
2 teaspoons (10 mL) pure vanilla extract
A pinch of sea salt

Combine the milk and parsnips in a medium saucepan. Bring to a full boil over medium heat. Cover tightly, remove from the heat, and let steep as the parsnip flavours the milk, at least 1 hour. Strain the mixture, pressing firmly to extract every drop. Transfer the milk to a high-speed blender. Add the cream cheese, sugar, vanilla, and salt. Purée until smooth. Refrigerate the mixture until cold. Transfer to an ice-cream maker and process according to the manufacturer's instructions. Transfer to an airtight container and freeze until set, at least 4 hours. Store for up to 1 week.

recipe continues

Serves 8

PREP AND PLAN
- Up to a week in advance, make the ice cream.
- The day before, make the Pumpkin Seed Brittle.
- On the day, make the Carrot Raisin Chutney and the Beet Paint, bake the cakes, assemble the components, and present the dessert.

Pumpkin Seed Brittle

This classic brittle relies on precise temperatures for success and pumpkin seeds for deliciousness.

Makes about 20 pieces

1 tablespoon (15 mL) butter, softened
1 teaspoon (5 mL) pure vanilla extract
½ teaspoon (2 mL) baking soda
Flaky sea salt
½ cup (125 mL) water
½ cup (125 mL) light corn syrup
1 cup (250 mL) sugar
1 cup (250 mL) salted roasted pumpkin seeds

Line a baking sheet with lightly oiled parchment paper or a silicone baking mat.

Measure the butter, vanilla, baking soda, and salt into a small bowl and reserve.

Pour the water and corn syrup into a large saucepan. Bring to a simmer over medium-high heat. Pour the sugar into the centre of the pan, being careful to avoid the edges. Continue cooking the syrup until a candy thermometer reads 285°F (140°C), then stir in the pumpkin seeds. Continue cooking until the mixture reaches 300°F (150°C). Remove from the heat and quickly stir in the butter mixture. Immediately pour the foaming brittle onto the prepared baking sheet. Cool completely. Break into pieces and store in an airtight container for up to 3 days.

Carrot Raisin Chutney

Sweet carrots easily absorb the bright spices of this chutney.

Makes 2 cups or so (500 mL)

1 tablespoon (15 mL) vegetable oil
2 cups (500 mL) peeled and finely diced carrots
    (about 12 ounces/340 g)
½ teaspoon (2 mL) cinnamon
¼ teaspoon (1 mL) nutmeg
¼ teaspoon (1 mL) ground allspice
¼ teaspoon (1 mL) ground cloves
1 cup (250 mL) dry white wine
1 tablespoon (15 mL) pure liquid honey
Zest and juice of 1 lemon
1 cup (250 mL) golden raisins

In a medium, heavy skillet, heat the vegetable oil over medium-high heat. Add the carrots and sauté until lightly browned. Add the cinnamon, nutmeg, allspice, and cloves and sauté a minute longer. Pour in the white wine, honey, and lemon zest and juice. Stir in the raisins, reduce the heat, and simmer until the carrots are tender and the mixture is syrupy, 10 minutes or so. Remove from the heat and reserve, or transfer to a container, cover tightly, and refrigerate for up to a week.

Beet Paint

Beets are deliciously sweet and easily puréed into this vivid sauce.

Makes about 2 cups (500 mL)

1 pound (450 g) red beets, trimmed, peeled, and diced
1 cup (250 mL) full-bodied dry red wine such as Cabernet Sauvignon, Shiraz, or Merlot
1 cup (250 mL) sugar

Measure the beets, red wine, and sugar into a large saucepan. Bring to a full simmer over medium heat, then reduce the heat to low, cover tightly, and simmer until the beets are soft, 15 minutes or so. Transfer to a high-speed blender and purée until smooth. Reserve or transfer to a container, cover tightly, and refrigerate for up to a week.

Rosemary Carrot Cakes

These classic carrot cakes are flavoured with complementary rosemary instead of the conventional spices.

Makes 8 individual cakes or 1 large cake

1½ cups (375 mL) all-purpose flour
1 cup (250 mL) tightly packed brown sugar
1½ teaspoons (7 mL) baking soda
1 teaspoon (5 mL) baking powder
½ teaspoon (2 mL) sea salt
2 tablespoons (30 mL) finely minced fresh rosemary
3 eggs
⅔ cup (150 mL) vegetable oil
2 teaspoons (10 mL) pure vanilla extract
2 cups (500 mL) peeled and shredded carrots

Preheat the oven to 350°F (180°C). Lightly oil and flour eight 6-ounce (175 mL) baking moulds or a 13 x 9-inch (3.5 L) baking pan.

In a large bowl, whisk together the flour, brown sugar, baking soda, baking powder, salt, and rosemary. In a small bowl, whisk together the eggs, vegetable oil, and vanilla. Stir the egg mixture into the flour mixture just until mixed. Stir in the carrots.

Divide the batter evenly among the moulds or scrape into the pan. Bake until a toothpick poked in the centre of the cake comes out clean, 20 minutes or so for individual cakes, 30 minutes for a single larger cake. Cool for a few minutes, then turn out onto a rack to cool completely, 30 minutes or so. Serve immediately, or store at room temperature in a tightly sealed plastic bag for up to 5 days, or freeze for 30 days.

PLATE AND PRESENTATION

- Dip a large pastry brush into the Beet Paint and brush a swoosh across the middle of the plate.
- Position a Rosemary Carrot Cake on the paint.
- Top the cake with a spoonful of Carrot Raisin Chutney.
- Nestle a scoop of Parsnip Cream Cheese Ice Cream alongside the cake.
- Top with a shard or two of Pumpkin Seed Brittle.

CHOCOLATE EXTRAVAGANZA

MILK CHOCOLATE MILK SAUCE, GIANDUJA FONDUE, RED HOT SAUCE, MANGO DROPS, COCOA CRUNCH, CHOCOLATE SORBET, MOLTEN DARK CHOCOLATE CAKES, WHITE CHOCOLATE WHIPPED CREAM

This memorable finish is meant for elaborately sharing. The spectacular presentation is anchored by old-school flavour, but really, it's just an excuse to rally your family and friends and enjoy an epic time together as you feast on every form of chocolate known to humans. You'll work hard to pull together the prep, but it'll be worth it for the memories. Though feel free to share the prep load and farm out a few of the various components to your family and friends in advance. Keep the details secret or entice them with wild promises of your edible vision.

Everyone gets to help present the flavours, build the show-stopping presentation, and then enjoy the works together. That's how to end a feast with a flourish.

Milk Chocolate Milk Sauce

This creamy sauce highlights the mild flavour of milk chocolate.

Makes 3 cups (750 mL)

1 cup (250 mL) whole milk
4 tablespoons (60 mL) butter
2 tablespoons (30 mL) brown sugar
1 tablespoon (15 mL) pure vanilla extract
12 ounces (340 g) milk chocolate, broken into small pieces

Measure the milk, butter, brown sugar, and vanilla into a small saucepan. Stir gently over medium heat until simmering. Remove from the heat and stir in the chocolate. Continue stirring until smooth and luxurious. Transfer to a 2-cup (500 mL) mason jar. Refrigerate until thoroughly cooled and thick, at least 2 hours or overnight. Store in an airtight container in the refrigerator for up to 5 days.

recipe continues

Serves 8

PREP AND PLAN

- Two or three days in advance, gather your various garnishes, find a bottle of chocolate liqueur, and prep as many of these components as you can: Milk Chocolate Milk Sauce, Gianduja Fondue, Red Hot Sauce, Mango Drops, Cocoa Crunch, Chocolate Sorbet, Molten Dark Chocolate Cake batter, and the White Chocolate Whipped Cream base.
- On the day, whip the white chocolate cream and bake the cakes.

Gianduja Fondue

Gianduja is a blend of chocolate and roasted hazelnut purée. Sound familiar? Look for the real thing, though: commercial versions pale in comparison and are far too sweet.

Makes 2 cups (500 mL)

1 cup (250 mL) heavy (35%) cream
8 ounces (225 g) gianduja chocolate
2 ounces Frangelico or other hazelnut liqueur

Pour the cream into a small saucepan. Stir over medium heat until simmering hot. Add the gianduja and liqueur. Continue stirring until melted and smooth. Transfer to 2 fondue bowls for sharing. Rest at room temperature or cover and refrigerate for up to 5 days.

Red Hot Sauce

This simple purée of raspberries adds an unexpected but pleasingly spicy twist to the presentation.

Makes 2 cups (500 mL)

1 cup (250 mL) red wine
½ cup (125 mL) sugar
1 tablespoon (15 mL) hot sauce
14 ounces (400 g) fresh or frozen raspberries
   (about 4 cups/1 L)

Measure the red wine, sugar, and hot sauce into a small saucepan. Bring to a slow, steady simmer over medium heat. Add the raspberries, return to a simmer, and continue cooking, stirring occasionally, until the fruit is soft, 5 minutes or so. Transfer to a high-speed blender and purée until smooth. Strain through a fine-mesh strainer, pressing firmly with the back of a ladle or spoon to remove the seeds. Refrigerate until cooled and thickened, about 1 hour. Cover tightly and store in the refrigerator for up to 5 days.

Mango Drops

A smooth purée of this tropical fruit is exotically tasty.

Makes 1 cup (250 mL)

1 large ripe mango, peeled, pitted, and diced
¼ cup (60 mL) Pernod, Sambuca, or other
   licorice-flavoured liqueur
Zest and juice of 1 lemon

Measure the mango, liqueur, and lemon zest and juice into a high-speed blender. Purée until smooth and silky. Transfer to a squeeze bottle or small bowl. Refrigerate for up to 5 days.

Cocoa Crunch

A few basic ingredients easily bake together for that crunch every dessert needs!

Makes about 1 cup (250 mL)

½ cup (125 mL) all-purpose flour
½ cup (125 mL) cocoa powder
½ cup (125 mL) sugar
6 tablespoons (90 mL) butter, frozen

Preheat the oven to 350°F (180°C). Line a baking sheet with lightly oiled parchment paper or a silicone baking mat.

In a medium bowl, whisk together the flour, cocoa powder, and sugar. Grate the butter into the mixture through the large holes of a box grater. Work the mixture into even clumps with your fingers. Spread evenly on the prepared baking sheet. Bake until crisp, 30 minutes. Rest on the baking sheet until cool. Store in an airtight container at room temperature for up to 5 days.

Chocolate Sorbet

This dairy-free treat is deeply flavoured with rich chocolate.

Makes about 4 cups (1 L)

1 cup (250 mL) cocoa powder
1 cup (250 mL) sugar
2½ cups (625 mL) water
1 teaspoon (5 mL) pure vanilla extract
¼ teaspoon (1 mL) sea salt
4 ounces (115 g) bittersweet chocolate, broken into small pieces

Measure the cocoa powder and sugar into a small saucepan. Gradually whisk in the water, just a splash at first, whisking until smooth before adding more. Whisk in the vanilla and salt. Whisking frequently, bring to a simmer over medium-high heat. Remove from the heat. Add the chocolate and rest for 5 minutes. Gently whisk until smooth. Refrigerate the mixture until cold and stable, overnight.

Transfer the mixture to an ice-cream maker and process according to the manufacturer's instructions. Serve immediately or freeze in an airtight container for up to a week.

White Chocolate Whipped Cream

Just when you thought whipped cream couldn't get any better, this version adds the rich flavour of white chocolate to the mix.

Makes 4 cups (1 L)

2 cups (500 mL) heavy (35%) cream, divided
8 ounces (225 g) white chocolate, broken into small pieces
1 teaspoon (5 mL) pure vanilla extract

Pour 1 cup (250 mL) of the cream into a small saucepan. Stir gently over medium heat until simmering. Add the white chocolate and vanilla and stir until smooth. Remove from the heat and rest until cool. Stir in the remaining 1 cup (250 mL) cream. Refrigerate until cold, 2 hours or overnight. Pour the mixture into the bowl of a stand mixer fitted with the whisk and whip until smooth. Serve immediately or refrigerate for up to an hour.

Molten Dark Chocolate Cakes

This classic remains my very favourite way to enjoy dark chocolate and is a spectacularly oozing way to anchor all the fun.

Makes 8 individual cakes

½ cup (125 mL) almond meal
¼ cup (60 mL) cocoa powder
¼ teaspoon (1 mL) fine sea salt
8 ounces (225 g) bittersweet chocolate, broken into small pieces
½ cup (125 mL) butter
1 teaspoon (5 mL) pure vanilla extract
4 eggs
¼ cup (60 mL) sugar

Preheat the oven to 400°F (200°C). Turn on the convection fan if you have one. Lightly butter eight 6-ounce (175 mL) ramekins or non-stick cake moulds. Sprinkle the moulds evenly with a heaping spoonful of white sugar, gently shaking, evenly coating, transferring the extra sugar to the next mould, and so on.

In a medium bowl, whisk together the almond meal, cocoa powder, and salt.

In a small saucepan, bring an inch or so of water to a simmer. In a medium metal bowl, combine the chocolate and butter. Place the bowl directly over the simmering water and stir gently until almost melted. Remove the bowl from the heat and continue stirring until smooth. Whisk in the vanilla and the almond meal mixture.

recipe continues

In a stand mixer fitted with the whisk, beat the eggs and sugar on high speed until smooth and thick. Gently stir in the chocolate mixture until evenly mixed. Divide the mixture evenly among the ramekins. (The filled ramekins can be covered and refrigerated overnight.) Place the ramekins on a baking sheet and bake until the top is firm and tender yet the interior is warm and gooey, precisely 7 minutes. Rest for 2 or 3 minutes, then invert and remove the ramekin. Serve immediately.

PLATE AND PRESENTATION

1 cup (250 mL) chocolate liqueur served in 8 mini (½-cup/125 mL) mason jars or festive shot glasses

Fresh raspberries or strawberries

Fresh herb sprigs, such as mint or anise hyssop, or edible flowers

Skewered marshmallows or crisp cookies for fondue dipping

A handful of small chocolate candies

- Lay a large sheet of glass or a large mirror on your table or ready a large food-safe surface. Pull the chairs away for best access.
- Organize all of the various dessert parts.
- Rally your friends and family and randomly assign everyone a component or two to add to the table.
- Bake the molten chocolate cakes and whip the cream.
- Take turns creatively adding the components to the presentation surface, scattering them here and there in an artistic fashion. Splash on the sauces first.
- Add the molten chocolate cakes.
- So they don't melt, finish with the whipped cream and frozen sorbet flourishes.

WILD BLUEBERRY MAPLE GRUNT

CARDAMOM DUMPLINGS, FRESH BASIL

On Prince Edward Island, if you get one or two country roads off the highway and go down some dirt lane, chances are you'll stumble onto a distinctive crimson-hued wild blueberry field. They are a wonderful addition to our agricultural landscape. Unlike their big bland berry-basket brethren (a high-bush blueberry hybrid grown year-round in warm climes), these wild northern plants grow low to the ground and produce smaller fruit with much more intense flavour. And lots of them. So many wild blueberries that Island cooks traditionally had enough to simmer into a delectable stew, often with maple syrup and bright lemon. Dumplings would then be baked or simmered in the stew. Our twist of fresh basil was not traditional, but if you try it once, you'll discover one of our favourite farm flavours for dessert. Blueberries and basil are delicious together, and cardamom loves basil too.

You can reliably find wild blueberries in the frozen fruit section of your favourite supermarket.

Make the Blueberry Stew

Preheat the oven to 350°F (180°C). Turn on the convection fan if you have one. (Alternatively, to cook on the stovetop, start the stew but instead of reducing it, add the dumplings, cover tightly, and simmer until they're tender and a toothpick inserted into the middle of a dumpling comes out clean, 15 minutes.)

Toss the blueberries, maple syrup, and lemon zest and juice into a large, heavy skillet. Bring to a full boil over medium heat and cook, stirring frequently, until thickened and reduced by half or so. Remove from the heat.

Make the Cardamom Dumplings

In a medium bowl, whisk together the flour, sugar, baking powder, and cardamom. Grate the butter into the mixture through the large holes of a box grater and evenly mix in the shards with your fingers. Pour in the milk and stir the mixture into a smooth dough. Using a spoon or your hands, divide the dough into 8 equal portions. Nestle the dough into the blueberry stew. Bake until the dumplings are tender and lightly browned, 20 minutes. Serve with lots of fresh basil sprinkled on top.

Serves 8

BLUEBERRY STEW
4 cups (1 L) fresh or frozen wild blueberries
1 cup (250 mL) pure maple syrup
Zest and juice of 1 lemon
Leaves from 1 bunch of fresh basil, tightly rolled and thinly sliced

CARDAMOM DUMPLINGS
2 cups (500 mL) all-purpose flour
¼ cup (60 mL) sugar
2 teaspoons (10 mL) baking powder
2 teaspoons (10 mL) ground cardamom
¼ cup (60 mL) butter, frozen
¾ cup (175 mL) whole milk

SKILLET APPLE CRISP

FIRE ICE CREAM, OATMEAL CRUST

During our fall apple season we're always inspired to make many different dishes both savoury and sweet. A freshly baked skillet full of classic apple crisp is one of my all-time favourites because it's such an inherent invitation to share. We love serving shared desserts, and encourage guest to serve themselves. Then we shock them with fiery hot ice cream made by stirring pure cinnamon oil into a standard ice cream base. The result is simultaneously chilly and fiery. Let's just say there's enough cinnamon in the ice cream for the whole dish.

Cinnamon oil can be found at specialty baking stores such as Bulk Barn and online.

Preheat the oven to 350°F (180°C). Turn on the convection fan if you have one.

Make the Fire Ice Cream

Pour the milk, cream, sugar, vanilla, salt, and cinnamon oil into a medium saucepan and, stirring to dissolve the sugar, bring to a simmer over medium heat. Beat the egg yolks together in a small bowl. Slowly whisk half or so of the hot cream mixture into the yolks. Stir the egg mixture back into the pot. Cook over low heat, stirring constantly, until the mixture thickens and reaches 175°F (80°C). Refrigerate the mixture until thoroughly chilled, 3 to 4 hours. Transfer the mixture to an ice-cream maker and process according to the manufacturer's instructions. Transfer to an airtight container and freeze until set, at least 4 hours. Store for up to 1 week.

Start the Skillet Apple Crisp

In a large bowl, toss the apples together evenly with the brown sugar, lemon zest and juice, and flour. Transfer to a large heavy skillet or large baking dish.

Make the Oatmeal Crust and Finish the Crisp

In a medium bowl, whisk together the oats, flour, and brown sugar. Grate the butter into the mixture through the large holes of a box grater and evenly mix in the shards with your fingers. Sprinkle the oatmeal mixture evenly over the apples. Bake until bubbly and browned, 1 hour.

Serves 6 to 8

FIRE ICE CREAM
1 cup (250 mL) whole milk
1 cup (250 mL) heavy (35%) cream
1 cup (250 mL) sugar
1 teaspoon (5 mL) pure vanilla extract
¼ teaspoon (1 mL) sea salt
¼ teaspoon (1 mL) cinnamon oil, more if desired
4 egg yolks

SKILLET APPLE CRISP
3 pounds (1.35 kg) tart apples (8 to 10 medium Cortland, McIntosh, Braeburn, or Granny Smith), unpeeled, cored and cut into chunks
½ cup (125 mL) tightly packed brown sugar
Zest and juice of 1 lemon
2 tablespoons (30 mL) all-purpose flour

OATMEAL CRUST
½ cup (125 mL) large-flake oats
½ cup (125 mL) all-purpose flour
½ cup (125 mL) tightly packed brown sugar
¼ pound (4 ounces/115 g) butter, frozen

CAMPFIRE MARSHMALLOWS

MOLASSES RUM

In the grand tradition of so many great restaurants, we offer our guests one last treat after dessert. What might be called a *mignardise*, a bite-sized dessert, in a classic kitchen is to us one more fire-inspired opportunity, a final taste to remember before guests fade into the night. An edible end to the story. What better way to end our epic FireWorks Feast than gathered around a flickering fire with friends old and new, dipping marshmallows in and out of the flames? Homemade marshmallows, of course! Preferably flavoured with the traditional sugar of every kitchen in Atlantic Canada. The treats brought back to us for so long by the ships we sent away full of fish. Molasses and the rum that was stowed away . . . Molasses rum marshmallows—an apt name. And as the flavours fade, we'll always remember the folks and stories around the campfire.

Make the Dusting Powder
Sift together the icing sugar and cornstarch in a small bowl. Lightly oil a 9-inch (2.5 L) square baking pan. Dust with some of the powdery mixture, reserving the rest for the marshmallows.

Make the Molasses Rum Marshmallows
In a small saucepan, bring an inch or so of water to a simmer. Pour the water into the bowl of a stand mixer. Sprinkle the gelatin over the water and stir it in as best you can. (It will look lumpy and grainy.) Let the mixture sit as it hydrates, 5 minutes or so. Place the mixer bowl directly over the simmering water and gently stir until the gelatin dissolves. Return the bowl to the mixer and fit it with the whisk.

Meanwhile, in a small saucepan combine the sugar, rum, corn syrup, molasses, and salt. Cook over medium heat, stirring occasionally as the sugar dissolves into a syrup. Continue as it simmers and rises in temperature. Wash down the sides occasionally with a moist pastry brush to keep crystals from forming. As soon as a candy thermometer reads exactly 245°F (118°C), remove from the heat.

With the mixer on medium speed, pour the hot syrup into the gelatin mixture in a thin, continuous stream between the whisk and the side of the bowl. Increase the speed to high and continue beating until the mixture is thick and fluffy but not too thick to spoon out, 10 minutes or so. Scrape the mixture into the prepared baking pan. Spread

Makes 16 large or 36 small marshmallows

DUSTING POWDER
½ cup (125 mL) icing sugar
½ cup (125 mL) cornstarch

MOLASSES RUM
MARSHMALLOWS
½ cup (125 mL) water
4 envelopes (1 ounce/28 g each) unflavoured plain gelatin powder (3 tablespoons/ 45 mL total)
2 cups (500 mL) sugar
½ cup (125 mL) dark rum
½ cup (125 mL) light corn syrup
¼ cup (60 mL) fancy dark molasses
¼ teaspoon (1 mL) sea salt

evenly with a lightly oiled spatula. Cool for an hour or so, then cover loosely with foil. Let rest at room temperature overnight to dry completely.

Lightly dust the marshmallows and your cutting board with some of the reserved dusting powder. Invert the pan and cut into squares with a sharp knife or kitchen scissors dusted with a bit more powder as you go: 3 cuts in each direction yields sixteen 2-inch (5 cm) square marshmallows, while 5 cuts in each direction will make 36 smaller ones. Generously dust the marshmallows with the remaining dusting powder. Store the marshmallows at room temperature between layers of parchment paper in an airtight container for up to 3 days.

Gather your friends and family, carve a few sticks, build a flickering fire, and toast away, dipping in and out of the flames until evenly toasted to your liking.

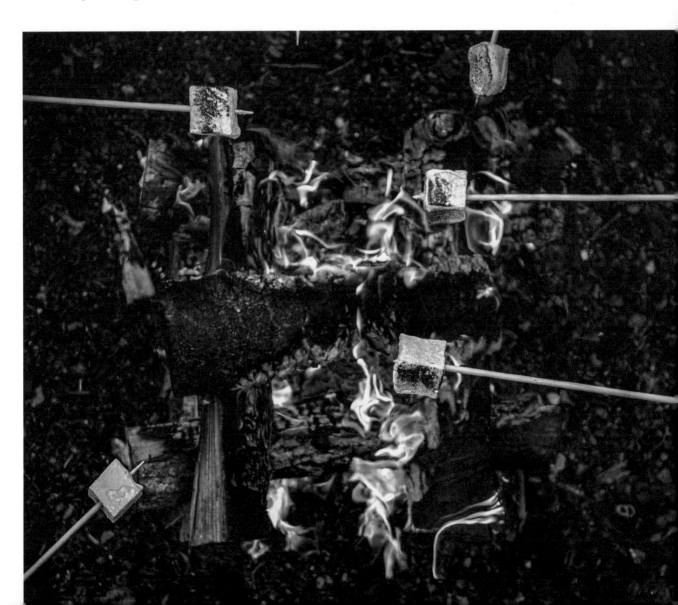

ROSE GIN

The molecules that give wild rose petals their intense fragrance are easily dissolved in various pure alcohols. That's the perfume business, and great news if you enjoy crafting farm-based cocktails like our Rose Gin Fizz (page 75). Be sure to pick over the wild rose petal for accidental insects.

Pack the rose petals into a 4-cup (1 L) mason jar. Pour in the gin. Seal tightly and let sit on the counter overnight. You'll be rewarded with a vivid liquid bouquet of rose flavour. Strain the gin through a fine-mesh strainer, pressing out every precious drop with the back of a spoon or ladle. Store in a festive bottle with your spirits until cocktail hour arrives and inspiration strikes.

Makes 26 ounces (750 mL)

4 ounces (115 g) freshly foraged wild rose petals from a fragrant unsprayed bush (about 4 loosely packed cups/1 L)

1 bottle (26 ounces/750 mL) of your favourite gin

SIMPLE SYRUP

This aptly named syrup has many uses, among them a simple way to sweeten a refreshing cocktail.

Measure the sugar and water into a small saucepan and cook over medium-high heat, stirring occasionally, until completely dissolved into a simmering syrup. Transfer to a 2-cup (500 mL) mason jar, seal tightly, and refrigerate until thickened and cool. Keeps for 1 month.

Makes about 2 cups (500 mL)

2 cups (500 mL) sugar
1 cup (250 mL) water

SPRUCE SALT

Salt preserves the intense fragrance of freshly picked spruce tips (see page 32). Use as a finishing salt over grilled meats, fish, and vegetables or as a curing salt for Hot-Smoked Salmon (page 91).

Makes 2 cups (500 mL)

1 cup (250 mL) freshly foraged spruce tips
2 cups (500 mL) kosher salt

———————

Toss the spruce tips and salt into a food processor and pulse, grinding just enough to evenly chop the tender spruce tips into the salt. Transfer to a 4-cup (1 L) mason jar. Tightly seal and store at room temperature until next year's crop emerges. Over time the fragrant salt will fade from bright green to muted orange, but its distinctive fragrance will endure.

APPLE RUM BUTTER

This traditional fruit preserve is packed with richly concentrated apple flavour mellowed with familiar spices and rum. It's an excellent and practical way to preserve the season's bounty for our future guests. Since apples are naturally sweet, this condiment is made without a lot of added sugar. Instead, long, slow simmering concentrates the fruit's sweetness far beyond regular applesauce. Along the way, rich flavour and smooth texture emerge.

Makes about 4 cups (1 L)

2 cups (500 mL) water
1 cup (250 mL) spiced rum
¼ cup (60 mL) freshly squeezed lemon juice
2 cups (500 mL) tightly packed brown sugar
1 teaspoon (5 mL) cinnamon
½ teaspoon (2 mL) ground allspice
½ teaspoon (2 mL) ground cloves
5 pounds (2.25 kg) apples (such as Honeycrisp, McIntosh, Cortland, Jonagold, Granny Smith), unpeeled, cored and quartered

———————

Preheat the oven to 300°F (150°C). Turn on your convection fan if you have one.

In a large pot, stir together the water, rum, lemon juice, brown sugar, cinnamon, allspice, and cloves. Stir in the apples. Bring to a boil, then reduce the heat, cover tightly, and simmer until the apples soften and collapse, 20 minutes or so. Purée until smooth with an immersion blender or in a food processor. Transfer the mixture to a large roasting pan. Bake, stirring every 30 minutes or so, until thickened, 3 hours or so.

LOBSTER BUTTER

Beyond the sweet, briny texture of lobster, the particular molecules that give this shellfish its distinctive marine flavour are easily dissolved in fat. They just need encouragement. For deeper lobster flavour you can re-infuse the butter several times with more shells.

Makes 4 cups (1 L)

2 pounds (900 g) leftover lobster shells, rinsed and drained
2 pounds (900 g) salted butter

Preheat the oven to 200°F (100°C).

Cover the shells with a kitchen towel and break into smaller pieces with a hammer. Melt the butter in a large ovenproof saucepan. Stir in the shells and continue heating just until the butter simmers. Remove from the heat, cover tightly, transfer to the oven, and bake for 8 hours.

Strain through a fine-mesh strainer. Repeat several times with more shells if desired, or transfer to a heatproof storage container. Refrigerate for up to 1 month or freeze indefinitely.

SEAWEED AIOLI

Here we infuse the classic mayonnaise of France with intensely flavourful seaweed powder. This rich condiment is brightly balanced and uniquely fragrant. It is an excellent condiment for any fish.

Makes about 1 cup (250 mL)

1 egg yolk
1 teaspoon (5 mL) Dijon mustard
¼ teaspoon (1 mL) sea salt
Zest of 1 lemon
2 tablespoons (30 mL) lemon juice
1 cup (250 mL) extra-virgin canola or olive oil, or your very best vegetable oil
1 or 2 tablespoons (15 or 30 mL) powdered dulse, nori, or other seaweed (see page 255).

Whisk together the egg yolk, mustard, salt, lemon zest, and lemon juice until thoroughly combined and frothy. Whisking continuously, slowly and steadily drizzle in the oil until a smooth, thick sauce emerges. Whisk in the seaweed. Serve immediately or cover tightly and refrigerate for up to 3 days.

RHUBARB CHUTNEY

This tangy condiment balances tart rhubarb with fiery ginger and bright star anise. Serve as a spicy sweet and sour sidekick for pork, chicken, fish, or vegetables.

———————

Measure the apple cider vinegar, brown sugar, ginger, and star anise into a large saucepan. Bring to a full boil over medium-high heat. Stir in the rhubarb and bring to a simmer. Reduce the heat and simmer, stirring frequently, until the mixture reduces and thickens, 20 minutes or so. Transfer to a 4-cup (1 L) mason jar or storage container. Tightly seal and refrigerate for up to 1 month.

Makes about 4 cups (1 L)

1 cup (250 mL) apple cider vinegar
1 cup (250 mL) tightly packed brown sugar
2 tablespoons (30 mL) grated frozen ginger
1 tablespoon (15 mL) ground star anise seeds
2 pounds (900 g) fresh rhubarb stalks, trimmed and cut into bite-sized chunks

TOMATO ANCHO CHUTNEY

A bright tomato condiment of balanced flavours, equally sweet, sour, spicy, and fragrant. The mid-level heat of smoky ancho chilies with fragrant coriander, fennel, and cumin adds lots of spicy Southwestern flavour.

———————

In a large pot, combine the red wine vinegar, sugar, chilies, tomato paste, coriander seeds, fennel seeds, cumin, garlic, bay leaf, and salt. Bring to a full boil over medium-high heat. Stir in the onions and bring to a simmer. Gently stir in the tomatoes, return to a full simmer, and simmer for 1 minute. Remove from the heat. Transfer the chutney to a mason jar or storage container. Tightly seal and refrigerate for up to 1 month.

Makes about 8 cups (2 L)

1½ cups (375 mL) red wine vinegar
¾ cup (175 mL) sugar
2 dried ancho chili peppers, stem discarded, broken into small pieces
2 tablespoons (30 mL) tomato paste
2 tablespoons (30 mL) coriander seeds
2 tablespoons (30 mL) fennel seeds
2 tablespoons (30 mL) ground cumin
4 garlic cloves, finely minced
1 bay leaf
1 teaspoon (5 mL) sea salt
1 large yellow onion, thinly sliced
3 pounds (1.35 kg) fresh ripe tomatoes, cut into bite-sized chunks

PERPETUAL SOUR CREAM

This sour cream harnesses the natural bacteria in our environment in the name of rich, tangy flavour and essential gut health.

Make the Starter Batch
Stir together the cream and buttermilk in a 4-cup (1 L) mason jar. Cover with a paper towel and secure by screwing on the ring band. Rest undisturbed at room temperature until the contents thicken noticeably, 24 hours or so. Enjoy immediately or replace the paper towel with the mason jar lid and refrigerate for up to 5 days.

When you're running low, make a new batch following the same procedure. In a clean mason jar, mix the new cream with ¼ cup (60 mL) of the previous sour cream. Cover with paper towel, secure with the ring band, and rest at room temperature until thickened.

Each batch makes 2 cups (500 mL)

STARTER BATCH
2 cups (500 mL) heavy (35%) cream
¼ cup (60 mL) buttermilk

EACH SUBSEQUENT BATCH
2 cups (500 mL) heavy (35%) cream
¼ cup (60 mL) of the previous batch of sour cream

STRAWBERRY CITRUS STEW

Sweet ripe strawberries swimming in juicy flavour, tasty from the bottom of our five-star breakfast Country Inn Granola Parfait (page 56) to the top of a five-star dessert. This simple barely-cook method encourages ripe berries to release their juices without damaging their flavour with prolonged heat.

Measure the strawberries, lime zest and juice, lemon zest and juice, and orange zest and juice into a saucepan. Stir together gently. Heat over medium heat, stirring occasionally, until evenly simmering, 5 minutes or so. Remove from the heat. Serve warm or refrigerate until lightly thickened. Store in an airtight container in the refrigerator for up to 5 days.

Makes 4 cups (1 L)

2 pounds (900 g) ripe hulled strawberries
Zest and juice of 1 lime
Zest and juice of 1 lemon
Zest and juice of 1 orange
1 cup (250 mL) sugar

FERMENTED TURNIP SLAW

The natural bacteria in our midst work their transformative magic on crisp turnip, transforming this humble root with an ancient technique and modern technology. You'll be amazed at how delicious the results are.

Makes 4 cups (1 L)

4 cups (1 L) peeled and coarsely shredded turnip
Fine sea salt

Place the shredded turnip in a medium vacuum bag. Weigh the bag of turnip on a digital scale. Calculate 2 percent of the weight, and add that weight of fine sea salt. Mix well.

Seal the bag with a vacuum sealer, sucking out all the air. Store in a cool, dark place, turning once a day to evenly distribute the contents. The bag will begin to inflate in a few days as nature takes it time transforming the turnip's earthy flavour. The salt helps regulate the natural process as the bag swells with fermenting gases.

After a full week, even two, when the bag seems about to burst, it's ready to open at last. It will smell horrible when you do. Persevere, though. Transfer the slaw to a 4-cup (1 L) mason jar or other storage container, tightly seal, and refrigerate for at least 2 days to allow the flavours to mellow. It will keep for up to a week.

PICKLED TURNIP SLAW

Crisply spicy raw turnips readily absorb this simple aromatic pickling liquid. Excellent on its own or tossed into other recipes.

Makes 4 cups (1 L)

4 cups (1 L) coarsely shredded peeled turnip (use a box grater)
1½ cups (375 mL) cider vinegar
1 cup (250 mL) sugar
½ cup (125 mL) water
2 tablespoons (30 mL) pickling spice
1 tablespoon (15 mL) sea salt

Pack the turnip into a 4-cup (1 L) mason jar. In a small saucepan, combine the cider vinegar, sugar, water, pickling spice, and salt. Bring to a boil over medium-high heat. Carefully pour the vinegar mixture over the turnip, patiently filling the jar. Seal tightly and refrigerate for up to a month. Alternatively, process with careful canning procedures until shelf-stable.

PICKLED RED ONIONS

The bright flavour and crisp texture of this ubiquitous condiment make it an excellent addition to many composed salads.

───────────────

Measure the red wine vinegar, sugar, and pickling spice into a large saucepan. Bring to a full boil over medium-high heat. Gently stir in the red onions. Cover tightly and remove from the heat. Rest at room temperature for 1 hour. Transfer to a 2-cup (500 mL) mason jar, seal, and refrigerate overnight. The picked onions are at their best after a few days of resting and will last up to a month.

Makes 2 cups (500 mL)

1 cup (250 mL) red wine vinegar
1 cup (250 mL) sugar
1 tablespoon (15 mL) pickling spice
2 or 3 thinly sliced red onions

SPECIAL INGREDIENTS AND CONTACTS

Many of the recipes in this book feature a specific ingredient from a particular supplier. In most cases a substitution is noted. If you're striving for authenticity, you can also contact the supplier directly.

Fortune Bay Oysters
Fortune, Prince Edward Island
fortunebayoysters.ca

Colville Bay Oysters
Souris, Prince Edward Island
colvillebayoysterco.com

Oyster Shucker
The Shucker Paddy
shuckerpaddy.ca
swissmar.com (for oyster knives)

Fresh Salmon
Sustainable Blue
Centre Burlington, Nova Scotia
sustainableblue.com

Afishionado
Halifax, Nova Scotia
afishionado.ca

Farm-Raised Halibut
Halibut PEI
Victoria, Prince Edward Island
halibutpei.ca

Afishionado
Halifax, Nova Scotia
afishionado.ca

Bluefin Tuna
TNT Tuna
Elmira, Prince Edward Island
tnttuna.com

Bottled Bar Clams
Annand Clams
Tyne Valley, Prince Edward Island
carla@annandclams.com

Seawater-Cooked Island Lobster
MR Seafoods
Charlottetown, Prince Edward Island
mrseafoods.com

Cold-Smoked Salmon
Oven Head Salmon Smokers
Bethel, New Brunswick
ovenheadsmokers.com

Glasgow Glen Farm Gouda Cheese
Glasgow Glen Farm
New Glasgow, Prince Edward Island
glasgowglenfarm.ca

Avonlea Farmhouse Clothbound Cheddar
Cows Creamery
Charlottetown, Prince Edward Island
cowscreamery.ca

Red Fife Whole-Grain Flour
Speerville Flour Mill
Speerville, New Brunswick
speervilleflourmill.ca

Cold Pressed Organic Canola Oil
Alpha Mills
Heatherdale, Prince Edward Island
alphamillsinc.com

Certified Island Beef
Atlantic Beef Products
Albany, Prince Edward Island
abpi.ca

Seaweed Powder
Plancton Marino
planctonmarino.com

Hana Tsunomata Edible Sea Vegetables
Acadian Seaplants
Dartmouth, Nova Scotia
acadianseaplants.com

THANK YOU

To Prince Edward Island and Canada beyond. To our Island home and to all who make it such a special place to cook. To our many hard-working farmers, fisherfolk, and culinary artisans. To the legendary Island way, our supportive community, and patient neighbours.

To chef Chris and farmer Kevin, thank you for embracing our farm and kitchen connection each and every day. Your leadership has taught us all so much.

To our dedicated staff, our service team, our Fire Brigade, the folks that work hard to share our vision, and to the families that support them. Each and every one of you give so much, all of us have built something truly special. Our best gets better every day.

To Chris, Kevin, and Al, this book wouldn't be what it is without each of you and all of us.

To my family. Gabe, Ariella, and Camille for loving your crazy dad and eating your vegetables. To my soulmate Chazz for inspiring, supporting, and driving me. (I love ya, babe!)

And to our guests. You inspire the hospitality in our soul. We're proud of our authentic best and humbled each and every day by your genuine support.

INDEX